DIRT!

DIRT!

THE PHILOSOPHY, TECHNIQUE, AND PRACTICE OF MOUNTAIN BIKING

John Howard

The Lyons Press

Printed in the United States of America

10 9 8 7 6 5 4 3 2 1

Design and composition by Rohani Design, Edmonds, Washington

Library of Congress Cataloging-in-Publication Data
Howard, John, 1947–
    Dirt!: the philosophy, technique, and practice of mountain biking
        / John Howard.
    p. cm.
    Includes index.
    ISBN 1-55821-530-1
    1. All terrain cycling. I. Title.
GV1056.H69 1997
796.6'3—dc21   97-17061
                                                                        CIP

CONTENTS

Taking Risks

Be still, my soul, be still; the arms you bear are brittle.

—A. E. Housman

OFF-ROAD AND OUT-OF-BODY—ATTITUDE, VISUALIZATION, AND TAKING CHANCES

Scholars of the ancient Chinese language report that two separate symbols in the vocabulary have precisely the same meaning. To our Western minds, those symbols—for crisis and opportunity—are as different as night and day, but to the ancient Chinese, they were one and the same. The English translation of these symbols reads: "Crisis is an opportunity riding the dangerous wind." This axiom might well be the perfect truth serum for gaining technical knowledge on a mountain bike.

Recently I was given an opportunity to challenge the dangerous wind and failed miserably. While pushing past my personal limits, I crashed and landed in the hospital. Strange how the mind works: While lying in a semiconscious lacerated heap, I never felt more alive. When I considered the whole of my life, that Chinese proverb made perfect sense. By re-evaluating every crisis as an opportunity we diffuse the bite of the pain and anguish of misfortune. After getting back on the bike a week later I realized this crisis had actually taken me a step higher on the technical ladder. A high price to pay for self-discovery? Perhaps, but it was still a step forward. Redefining a crisis brought me face to face with the core of my feelings about why I rode and raced mountain bikes in the first place.

This book was written (or ridden) for everyone who rides, or has even thought of riding, a mountain bike—from pure recreational weekenders to hard-core racers and including all of us Walter Mitty competitors in between. To all of you who fantasize about escaping the grid of cement and asphalt, traffic and air pollution, this lesson plan is for you: You'll learn a few basic tricks, push your personal limits, and have fun in the process. The old Chinese warlords must have learned two thousand years ago to laugh in the face of devastation and cry from the joy of being alive. In both cases the end result is the kind of enlightenment that makes us grateful for simple blessings like blue sky and fresh air.

If you are just getting started, rest assured that this book is not going to rush you toward ripping, shredding, or even breaking the gravitational bounds of earth. In fact I'd like to begin by replacing the popular image of hell-bent mountain biking with one of judicious self-preservation. According to demographics, most mountain bikes spend their time on pavement or gathering dust in garages rather than on dirt trails. It is my hope that this narrative will inspire the dirt devil lurking in each of you. Take heart: Some of the most seemingly fearless off-roaders had road-bike or no-bike beginnings. In short, it is never to late to rediscover your childhood on a mountain bike. Whatever your bike means to you, start with a fresh attitude about using it as a tool for self-exploration.

For those readers who are advanced kamikaze edge players, let this book serve as a mission statement to the wise: Keep on challenging yourself with every adventure that the forces of sport and life may throw in your path, but remember, risk ventures fall roughly into two categories: *calculated* and *uncalculated*. Do yourself and the sport a favor: Aim for the former and respect the latter. The next time you go flat-out down a killer descent, try to keep clear in your mind which form of risk fits your present situation. Most of you are extremely goal-driven animals. The competitive spirit that brought your gonzo spirits to the trail to test yourself against others of the same ilk hardens you to the element of risk.

If you are a beginner, you should be here not to test the edges of your limits but merely to play. An early goal should be to cultivate the art of the instinctive response. It may seem like a gross oversimplification, but this natural human resource will allow you to push aside the limiting effects of fear and doubt. Once you are motivated by desire rather than fear, the trail is yours. Out of desire, we respond naturally to every condition the trail throws our way. Downhill mountain-bike racers can learn a lot by watching practiced downhill skiers. In both cases, the athlete learns to anticipate several moves ahead of the most visible object in the route.

Experienced mountain bikers and skiers usually test a particular course by "prerunning" it again and again before actually hitting it at racing speeds. This means they imagine themselves performing smoothly and quickly over difficult course conditions and visually reinforce these positive images. On a difficult technical section, start by parking your bike and walking. Course conditions may seem intimidating at first, but by going over and familiarizing yourself with the terrain, you can visualize a positive image of yourself in motion. As you walk, mentally and physically work yourself through a technical move until you are comfortable with the conditions. Before you get on your bike, close your eyes and mentally retrace every bump. Now you are ready to ride. Notice how effortless and smooth the same particular set of conditions seems. Your learning curve will increase dramatically if you learn to enjoy each ride. All advancements in technical skill will come about only when the body is relaxed. Remember, you're here to have fun.

HONING AN ATTITUDE

Mountain-bike riders can be divided into two categories, depending on age: BMX era and pre-BMX era. Bicycle motocross (BMX) started with kids mimicking motorcycle motocross racing and grew into a serious sport worldwide. Those of us over thirty-five who were stuck in Little League or other sports commitments and missed BMX are forced to hone our balance, coordination, and reflexes by playing catch-up with gravity.

For you older riders and the rest of the pack who landed in other sports or other commitments, you'll have to learn to loosen up. Most of us who come from a road-bike background hold ourselves in a rigid, unbending stance while riding. Stay loose and keep your body in a constant state of fluid animation. Frustration and anxiety are not emotions you want to bring with you when you ride. As soon as the ride ceases to be fun, you might as well hang up your bike, because you are no longer learning anything.

The first thing to remember about relaxing is to avoid the tendency to hold your breath. Breathe deeply with a controlled rhythmic pattern of out-breaths. Try to time your exhaled breaths with the rise and fall of the cranks and the flow of the terrain. Once in motion, take a moment to flap your elbows and legs as you descend. This will help loosen your body.

The best way to make the lessons learned on a trail stick is to analyze a particular trail's conditions and determine a realistic, progressive course of action. Decide in advance, for example, how you're going to scramble up that steep slope, or that you'll use a rock in the middle of the trail for a ramp to get air. Try not to even think of such things as obstacles; they are, rather, conditions of nature. You did not come to the woods to conquer nature; you came instead to co-exist with it. When you fail—and we all fail—try again. Let's say you're attempting to jump a particular log, and that maybe you've tried a couple of times to get over the thing without success. Rather than accept the frustration of failure, step back and downscale to a slightly smaller log, and proceed. When you succeed with the smaller log, reinforce the successful procedure several times to boost your confidence. Always prerun a particularly difficult section of terrain or a particular task, like jumping the log. Always build your confidence by repeating something you did well several times before moving on to the next obstacle. For most of us, progress comes from combining self-analysis, observation, and a healthy respect for our own personal learning curves.

What this is not about is your or anyone else's relative "talent." The world is full of unrewarded talent, and we shouldn't be concerned with such ambiguities. Focus instead on having fun, and the rest will follow. I recommend riding with and imitating experienced partners; just make sure you don't try to progress too rapidly. My first experience with learning to ski taught me about that pitfall. I was progressing nicely with the other beginners on my little skis until my more experienced friends challenged me. With more ego than brains I abandoned the didactic lessons and notched up the ladder in leaps and bounds. The results were predictable: I ended up tackling slopes I wasn't yet ready for, failing, and losing valuable self-confidence, which reduced my learning curve to crawl speed.

A better approach would have been to constantly make mental notes of my friends' methods and repeat their techniques on my own, gradually taking the degree of difficulty a bit farther each time. Pushing the envelope of adventure does not mean your mistakes have to be paid for in flesh and blood. Progressing slowly may require a bit more patience, but it means you will be less likely to take self-destructive risks.

This methodical progressive technique helped me safely set the bicycle speed record of 152 mph. Later, a challenger who attempted to break the record by progressing too quickly broke thirteen bones instead. Just as imitation and slow progression are important for learning radical techniques, a fair amount of experimental solo trial-and-error riding is a must if you want to reinforce good results. You may fail, but remember: Failure isn't fatal; nor is success forever. If you fall, big deal—get up and try it again until you get it right.

If you are just breaking ground with mountain bikes, learning to descend is going to be a time you will never forget, a sort of reacquaintance with your primal self. You can look forward to returning home tired and dirty, maybe even a bit scraped, but—more important—you will feel good about yourself. This is a fun sport, and after you have traversed the element of defeat a few times the fun will come in spades.

CHAPTER 1

The Lay of the Land

WHAT THE TRAIL HAS TO OFFER

Every trail has its own unique character marked with features, not unlike a good bottle of wine. Some are gentle and forgiving, while others are less mellow and sometimes carry a bite. Below are a few types, terms, and conditions that define the trail.

TRAIL TYPES AND TERMS

FIRE TRAIL (JEEP OR TRUCK TRAIL): Usually wide enough for several riders to ride side by side. A broad graded track wide enough for two or three riders or two twin single tracks an axle apart are common. If the trail is well used by pedestrians, horses, or bikes, one track will be faster and better groomed than the other.

Fire Trail

SINGLE TRACK: Everyone's favorite one-lane personal trail. These may also be occupied by hikers and equestrians, so, as always, a key point is "shared usage."

Single Track

FASTEST OR BEST LINE: The smoothest ridable path on a trail.

CROWN: Usually the high middle ground and often a rough transition between paths.

WASHOUT (OR RUT): A gully usually created by soil erosion. Washouts pose a serious threat or a great challenge to MTBers. Caused by storm damage, they often run the length of a trail. Get to know them and don't let them ruin your day. There is no universal rule on successful negotiation of ruts, but most of us agree they should be avoided.

Washout.

BERM (BAR): A mound in the trail worn from erosion and continual use; occasionally you'll find man-made berms, built to arrest erosion. The man-made versions are sometimes referred to as water bars. The man-made berm in the photo allows you to bank off a turn to facilitate your entry and exit. On flats and downhill sections, berms are great for jumping. They are a cyclist's answer to moguls on a ski run.

ROCKS, ROOTS, AND LOOSE TREE LIMBS: Avoid
them if they pose a threat, or use them to heighten your fun.
Learn to trust your intuition.

HIGH SIDE–LOW SIDE: Trails are often dug into the sloping sides of hills, so they sometimes have a high, or uphill, side and a low, or downhill, portion.

SURFACE CONDITIONS

Surface conditions are always changing, as they are influenced by nature and the whims of man. A well-rounded rider responds instinctively to ever-changing course conditions, from mud to ice and from sand to water.

Mud. The best way to deal with mud is to power through it by maintaining momentum and pedaling. Applying power with lots of rpms, low gears, and plenty of momentum is always the best approach. If your speed begins to drop, try balancing your weight back and staying off the front wheel, which tends to dig in if overweighed. Steer as straight and as little as possible. Most of us get into trouble when the front wheel starts bobbing back and forth and plowing at slow speeds—so keep your speed up. Given a choice of tires for muddy conditions, pick a thinner width with sparse tread that will spit off the globs of ooze with minimum sticking. Wider treads simply pick up more mud. Tire pressure is also a factor. For maximum traction I recommend running five to ten pounds less pressure than you would normally run for hard, dry conditions. Given a choice of a wet puddle versus a gooey one, opt for the wet. The water will help loosen the muck and clean off some of the existing mud. Local pro rider Steve Kinney recommends waxing the entire bike—tires, frame, and all. As for the wax, my personal favorites include the commercial cooking product Pam and a new, well-tested product called Mudd Off. Spray your bike down with either of these products before a particularly muddy ride or race and you will find yourself tugging around a few less pounds of turf.

Water. The usual encounter with water occurs during a stream crossing. Use caution on unfamiliar crossings where depth is questionable. In fact, the rule is that if you can't see the bottom, or the stream crossing comes early in your ride, portage the bike and save the wear and tear on the drivetrain. If you decide to go for it, look for the tracking lines of other bikes. Also watch for ripples, which indicate large submerged objects. Pick an appropriate gear; lower gears are usually a good idea for deeper water. Just as with mud, pedaling momentum is critical. Keep your weight as far back as possible to "float" the front wheel over submerged obstacles. Since brakes usually take a while to activate on wet rims, you may want to dry them by "feathering"* the brakes upon exiting the water. If you know ahead of time that you are going to be encountering wet conditions, make sure to have some extra wet-condition lube on your chain to avoid further deterioration of the drivetrain. A tip on preventive maintenance: I suggest sealing some of the lower frame vents in your steel frame with electrician's tape or clear silicone to keep the water out of the tubes.

Sand. Here is where the fat tires really prove their worth, especially on the front. Lower tire pressure is also helpful in getting through deeper conditions. On rapid sandy downhills, keep your steering straight and your weight back. Make *very* subtle steering adjustments. How many times have I watched downhillers trying to negotiate fast, deep sand sections with utter abandon? Those who prevail usually do so by sliding back in the saddle and "floating" the front wheel rather than reducing

* *"Feathering" means activating the rear brake enough to semilock the wheel while giving simultaneous light dabs on the front wheel.*

speed. On flat ground stay seated with your weight evenly distributed, both front and back and side to side. As with mud, sit back and power through with lots of torque, and remember to keep that front wheel straight. A canted front wheel digs into the sand with the same relative effectiveness as a brake.

Rock. The most common rock conditions found on many trails include clusters of small rocks that are best ridden through and around rather than over. Conditions will dictate technique. Shift your body weight and gears to "ebb and flow" over the rocks. On difficult, steep, or rocky climbs, stay forward as long as possible. On stable, nonshifting rock faces, keep the pedal pressure steady and your weight back so you can pop the front wheel up and over those less friendly stony wheel grabbers. Bar ends are a real godsend for this purpose. For scrambling over large smooth rock sheets like the famous slickrock at Moab, the most important consideration is rear-wheel traction. The fatter, softer compound knobbies and slick-surface tires are good choices for this purpose. Slightly lower pressures are the norm on rocky surfaces, but be careful of the mountain biker's most common problem, the "snakebite" (twin-prick) punctures from rough-and-tumble downgrades, which tend to compress the tires and tubes against the rims.

Snow. Despite having only two wheels, mountain bikes are amazingly adept at traversing different consistencies of snow and even ice. Bike builder Turner Drive of Rogers, Arkansas, has a very well-engineered flex drive bike, which can operate conventionally or with two-wheel drive; he also makes an adapter kit for your present bike that will vastly increase traction in the slick stuff. Accessory manufacturers offer mountain-bike tire chains and even metal-studded tires for more extreme conditions. Dan Hanibrink of Big Bear, California, builds an incredibly stable eight-inch-wide treaded all-terrain bike for extreme conditions such as deep snow, slick ice, or heavy sand. Winter mountain biking on slick conditions, despite the obvious dangers, is still one of the best ways to improve your overall balance and handling techniques. Just as when driving a car, make your turns wider, stop sooner, and remember to steer in the direction of the slide. As a matter of interest, several European cyclists have actually exceeded 100 mph while barreling down well-packed ski slopes on specially prepared mountain bikes.

Dust. Riding in thick, choking dust behind a huge pack of MTBers may not sound like much fun, but, hey, think about all those minerals you'll be ingesting. If you find yourself in this situation on unfamiliar ground, back off on your speed and relax. I've seen ugly and unnecessary crashes in races because some riders got overly anxious and tried to pass when they couldn't see the trail in front of them. Clear eye shades or, if conditions are really bad, goggles are usually the best way to keep the stuff out of your eyes. An increasingly popular product for mass-start, dirty conditions is the painter's mask, which keeps your airway clean when the air is not.

SHARING THE TRAIL WITH HIKERS AND EQUESTRIANS

Politically correct behavior is especially important in this period of mountain biking's restless infancy. As popular trails become more crowded and land available for usage shrinks, common sense dictates being considerate to both pedestrians and horseback riders. Of the three interest groups, we bikers are definitely on the shakiest ground by virtue of our "new kid on the block" status. Give special thought to future generations of trail riders, who may be legislated right off the trail if we take too much for granted.

Always give hikers and horses plenty of distance, and be friendly. Let them know how many are in your party and how soon they can expect to see the others. On narrow trails, it is always a good idea to slow down when approaching hikers. As for horses, even on a wide fire road, make it a habit to dismount completely in the presence of a horse or horses until you get some feedback from the rider. This will signal concern for their welfare and keep the horsefolk on our side.

Note: International Mountain Bicycling Association (IMBA) is a non-profit advocacy organization dedicated to promoting mountain bicycling that is environmentally sound and socially responsible. Their "Rules of the Trail" have been recognized around the world as the simple, essential code of conduct for off-road cyclists. For more information write: IMBA, P.O. Box 7578, Boulder, CO, 80306-7578.

CHAPTER 2

Performance Positioning

In our training schools* we use a computerized interactive-TV training system known as the CompuTrainer to test power output for our athletes. We have discovered that correctly positioned riders can improve their power output by as much as 35 percent, and on average by about 12 percent. Generally speaking, the higher the seat, the more powerful the position. Still, effective positioning sometimes involves making compromises. For example, if a cyclist has tight external hip rotators or iliotibial bands, he or she will never be able to fully utilize the more powerful position. Here are a few of the parameters to keep in mind.

SADDLE

A lower saddle position is preferred for beginners. In order to make your life a bit easier, equip your bike with a quick-release seat post. When sitting on the bike with your feet on the pedals (pedals should be in the 12 and 6 o'clock positions), your leg extension angle should be about 50 to 60 degrees (between thigh and calf on the leg in the 6 o'clock pedal). This is a good position for gaining confidence, but it won't produce much power. With this seat height, you should be able to comfortably touch the ground with your feet. Later on, to get maximum power, gradually slide the seat up a full inch and a half to two inches. Ultimately, the goal is a leg angle of about 35 to 40 degrees at the bottom, or 6 o'clock, position, with a slight toe-down angle of the foot.

A fairly simple method for arriving at 35 degrees is to sit squarely on the saddle and grip the bars. (Have someone hold

*School of Champions

Optimum power and stability are inversely proportional. At this saddle height the rider achieves a 35-degree angle at the bottom of the stroke, a ballpark maximum for cross-country riding.

your bike upright or use a training stand to secure it.) With the leg locked at the knee, and your hips even, your saddle should be high enough for the heel of your mountain-bike shoe to barely touch the 6 o'clock pedal. In our schools, we find that people who frequently ride with too-low saddles sometimes experience knee pain when they raise the saddle to the correct height. For this reason, I suggest raising the saddle in small increments to avoid sudden changes of force on the knees. Generally, the lower saddle positions will exert more force on the knees. The 30- to 35-degree angle allows you to utilize more of your natural strength from the big muscles of the lower body. (By the way, next to the collarbone, the knees are the weakest point in a cyclist's body.) For training and racing, experienced cross-country riders typically keep their saddles up for more climbing and flat-land power, while downhillers lower their saddles and sacrifice power for control and stability. Every situation and every body is different; get to know your limits for various turf conditions.

The fore and aft adjustment of the saddle should allow for a comfortable flattening of the back with the elbows bent. Comfort, performance, and length of upper torso will dictate saddle placement and handlebar stem length. If a mountain biker is sitting too far back or the bars are too far away, he or she will not be able to exert much leverage while climbing. Body position is also a key factor in downhill stability. If the same rider is too far forward, either because of saddle adjustment or an extra-long handlebar stem, safety will be compromised when the trail gets steep. If the frame and corresponding top tube are correctly chosen, the saddle will be set toward the middle of the saddle rails. However, if you have a short upper torso and arms, you'll need a slightly forward seat and, perhaps, a shorter handlebar stem. Remember, if your top-tube-and-stem combination is too long, you may have difficulty sliding your butt back over the saddle on a steep descent. As a last point, the nose of the saddle should be level.

Save yourself the hassle of an Allen key adjustment and fit a quick-release binder bolt to your frame.

BARS AND STEMS

The height and reach of your handlebars is determined not only by the length of the handlebar stem but also by the pitch. Ideally, you should be able to comfortably flatten your back when riding. This in turn leads to more relaxed controlled breathing. If you find yourself straining to reach the bars or going anaerobic a shade sooner than you like, the solution may be to raise your bars.

The problem with raising the bars of better-quality mountain bikes is that the modern head assemblies no longer use expander bolt stems. They're designed to be extra long so that riders can customize fit by cutting off the excess. This means that in order to preserve some adjustability you should probably pack a few spacer washers on the steering tube before you or your mechanic whack the steering tube off too short. I've seen mountain bikers put themselves through some serious self-flagellation as a result of chopping their steering tubes too short. The resulting neck pain and less-than-optimum position can seriously compromise your ability to transfer oxygen, and your performance will suffer.

Perhaps a word of caution might be in order to those shopping for a new bike: Before going for a test ride, adjust the seat up to that 35- to 40-degree "power" position. When you test-ride the bike, punch the pedals a few times to make sure there is a sufficient amount of seat tube for power and comfort. Make sure you can get your back flat. If you think you may already be too low on your present bike, you may need to look for a stem with more upward pitch.

When you get right down to it, the most efficient cross-country position looks a lot like a well-balanced road fit.

You've probably never even heard of the goniometer—essentially, a protractor that measures leg angle. No sweat: Just adjust the pedal straight down, lock the leg, square the hips on the saddle, and the heel should be even with the pedal.

BAR EXTENSIONS

Not just cool accessories, these add-ons allow you to exert greater upper-body force and a wider stance when climbing, especially on steep, out-of-the-saddle grades. Bar extensions need to be positioned so you can easily grab them and leverage more power both in and out of the saddle. They are also great for supporting the bike during upside-down drivetrain maintenance and cleaning.

SHOES AND PEDAL ADJUSTMENTS

For cross-country, use mountain-bike shoes rather than running shoes. Firm-soled shoes will protect your knees and will add a good deal of power to your stroke. SPD pedals with a degree of free float are the now the industry standard. Some purists still use clips and straps, and of course they come standard on lower-priced bikes, but for anyone who is experiencing knee pain I recommend a modern free-floating pedal system.

The biggest advantage to a good free-floating system is that the shoe rotates on the shoe cleat, thus transferring the primary pedal load from the critical knee joint to the big lower-body muscles, such as the quads, glutes, and hamstrings. This foot rotation allows the muscles and joints to assume a more natural range of motion.

Nonfloating pedal systems and clip systems with lateral adjustment should mimic your natural foot plant. Fore and aft adjustment should find the ball of your foot slightly forward of the pedal axle. The deeper (cleat back, foot forward) foot positions allow you to generate more power and leverage.

CHAPTER 3

Braking

WHEN TO BRAKE, WHEN TO NOT . . .

It seems appropriate to learn braking techniques first. Beginners just starting to get dirty should practice the art of stopping as a prereqisite skill to cornering and descending. Brakes, however, are a double-edged sword: They save our lives routinely, but they can also get us into deep trouble with the same degree of regularity. Novice riders, and some avid cyclists who should know better, sometimes nail their brakes in moments of uncertainty. This overuse syndrome slowly diminishes as specific trails become more familiar and skills improve. As you ride, reinforce the practice of extra-light feather braking. From this you will learn the art of precise control. Smooth, controlled braking is a matter of constant practice, with the end result being as automatic as Pavlov's salivating dog.

Start by knowing which hand operates which brake. It sounds stupid, but a lot of beginners don't know the difference. The right hand controls the rear wheel, and the left controls the front. Another consideration is mechanical adjustment. As a rule, the lever adjustment should be firm and powerful, with good stops executed using only the index fingers of both hands. This way you have more fingers controlling the bike. Learning the exact percentages of front-brake versus rear-brake bias on a given trail means finding your limits under every possible condition the trail offers. Even if you are using a pair of the latest power clampers, like Shimano's V-brakes or maybe a disc or hydraulics, the amount of pressure is still determined by the number of fingers applied on the levers.

Instinctive behavior developed by relentless practice counts for a lot in braking. Many times, determining the precise moment and applying exact amount of braking will take place so quickly that conscious thought would have simply gotten in the way. You should develop a keen sense of the limitations of your brakes. Consider such factors as surface conditions of the turf or trail, relative speed, rim conditions (dry or wet), and the adjustment of the brake handles—tight handles will stop you faster, but some of us prefer a slightly looser front handle to avoid overbraking the front wheel. Don't learn the hard way that you have to stay light or completely off the front brake in moments of marginal control, like on steep descents. You can get hurt by locking the front brake on a steep drop and having your front wheel slide out from under you. The other classic mistake is the ever-painful endo—a head-over-handlebars tumble—which is usually a result of both an overzealous front brake and too much weight forward, causing the rider to flip over the bars quicker than a broken promise. Sometimes keeping your hand planted on the grip and well clear of the front brake can be enough to help you plow through a turn or get you down a monster downgrade with only a rear brake. You also have to weigh the larger concern for the enviromental impact of sliding the rear knobbie all the way to the bottom.

HOT STOPS

In our School of Champions camps and clinics we practice a method of controlled "hot stopping," or controlled panic braking, which can save a rider in the face of a collision. The fact is that sooner or later you are going to find yourself in a situation where you will need to avoid an imminent crash by stopping your bike faster than normal. Since most mountain bikes, like most four-wheel-drive vehicles, see more use on the street than they they do on the trail, you need to be prepared when that minivan full of screaming kids suddenly pulls directly into your path. Don't blame the driver; on the trail, trees and large rocks have been known to do the same thing.

Hot stopping requires you to adjust your weight immediately to the rear of the saddle, then plant about two-thirds of your braking pressure on the front brake. The object is to get most of your weight back on the rear wheel to facilitate braking while avoiding skidding either wheel and keeping the bike straight. Done correctly, this should require only about half your normal stopping distance. Obviously, the firmness of the turf will determine the amount of rear versus front bias. At the first sign of trouble, adjust your weight back over the saddle in the "ready" mode.

To make this technique a regular part of your defensive arsenal, practice it over and over until it becomes second nature. Then, heaven forbid, if the real emergency comes looking for you, the safe response will be instinctive.

Once you have the hot stop down, you will want to try a variation on the same theme. This practice routine involves the application of front-wheel-only braking, a technique I call "nose braking." This exaggerated technique helps you learn about balance and the effects of controlled weight distribution. It will also help improve your reaction time. Start rolling along slowly on firm ground; on cue, you will simultaneously slide your weight slightly to the rear (but not as far back as you would for the hot stop) and apply modulated pressure to the front wheel. With this technique the back wheel comes off the ground. Success involves split-second timing of brake pressure and how quickly you can transfer your weight. Your goal should be to get com-fortable with the rear wheel six to eight inches off the ground.

Quicker than an oooooshi—get back on the rear wheel and nail that front brake harder than the rear. The bike will do its part by cutting the stopping time in half. The rear wheel off the ground is a more advanced and completely optional technique.

TO LOCK OR NOT TO LOCK

On a super-steep downgrade, you will eventually find yourself in a situation where maximum braking force (as in locking up and sliding the rear wheel) is the fastest and safest method for getting down the hill. This technique involves two separate practice sessions. The first will be on a steep descent with your weight well back over the rear wheel and minimum steering input. The second involves locking on a flat or a slight downgrade. You will begin the slide and then steer in the direction of the skid.

A big problem with practicing this type of lockup braking (where the rear tire is completely locked) is that in no time it will seriously deteriorate a trail. On delicate wash-prone trails, we should place damage control above the simple thrill and challenge of traversing a big descent. I have arrived at big races two days early to test the course, only to find the layout of unstable technical sections completely different on race day!

On most of the groomed trails in this country, it is environmentally wrong to lock and slide. Also, common sense dictates that sliding wheels means the bike may be escaping your control. Many, many crashes occur because of braking at the wrong time. For these reasons, I suggest getting in the habit of looking for alternative methods of braking on a downhill, including steering and even pedaling through downhill turns. Always look for a berm or bank to carve* before you shred.† Having said this, I will also say there will be times when fine-tuning your limits with an occasional prudent and well-timed rear skid and turn is the best approach. Locking near the entry of a turn will help give you traction control and set you up for achieving the perfect line

*A carve is a rapidly executed turn usually involving a hard, banked movement. We often speak of carving banked turns, meaning to ride them high, then cut back to the trail with minimal loss of speed.
†Shred: The meaning of this term has evolved from the not-exactly-environmentally-friendly practice of tearing and ripping the earth—with or without braking—to simply executing a radical move. Sometimes aerial maneuvers are referred to as shredding.

of entry and exit on a turn. While you certainly want to avoid locking on sensitive wash-plagued trails, I recommend practicing controlled tire-ripping skids whenever conditions allow. (Contrary to what you may be thinking, I receive no kickbacks from any tire manufacturers for recommending this.)

I started shredding way before anyone was cycling on dirt. When I was a kid, my younger brother and I used to wet down our polished driveway and garage with a garden hose and come in hot, locked, and drifting on our middleweight 1950s cruisers. Virtually all of my early MTB training came from these experiences. While I can't recommend this practice today, it did dredge up some fond memories the first time I locked up and threw dirt.

Find yourself a nonendangered trail or some smooth, packed dirt or a packed sandy section and practice this lock-

The rule is, Always shred lightly, and don't try this in your favorite national forest.

and-slide maneuver until you can execute a full 180-degree slide to both the left and the right. The rule is, Always shred lightly.

TIRE PRESSURE

Correct tire pressure is an important element of effective braking, cornering, and general trail stability. I've been at NORBA (National Off Road Bicycle Association) races in the rain where a good percentage of the downhill or slalom field would puncture from treading too fine a line between vital traction and snakebitten tubes resulting from too little air. Talk to the more experienced pros and experts and discover what tire pressure they are running for a given course condition. Then remember that, ultimately, tire pressure has to be set by individual body weight. Try low pressure on one run and higher pressure on the next until you run out of tubes, or feel the difference in terms of grab.

The same procedure should also be used when riding cross-country. In dry conditions, overinflated tires can cause real stability and traction problems. In muddy conditions, once the tread is completely caked smooth with mud there will be virtually no traction. In wet mud, a lower-pressure tire will form a slightly wider footprint and thus bite the muck more predictably.

Occasionally even you hard-cores have to ride your mountain bikes on paved roads. For these rides, more tire pressure is advisable to avoid energy-sapping scrub—wasted motion caused by too much tread for the conditions and/or sidewall flex from insufficient tire pressure—which naturally occurs, especially when riding out of the saddle. Your best bet is wide

Whenever you check your tires with a gauge, get into the habit of feeling the side-wall pressure—for the times you may not have a gauge handy.

center-ridge tires or, better yet, a pair of baldie road tires, perhaps mounted on a separate set of wheels for "road days."

As a footnote, Juliana Furtado and a host of other NORBA pros do much of their training on the road.

LOOSE GRIPS

When the going gets rough, good brake and bike control depend on secure handlebar grips. A common problem in hot, sticky weather when you are also sweating up a storm is grip slippage: One or both grips become contaminated and begin giving way in midride. Often with no warning they start freefloating on the bars. This is no fun at all and will result in considerable cursing, as well as diminished control, if not corrected. A foolproof method of keeping grips tight is to remove them before you ride and thoroughly dry them and the bars. Then push them back on with hair spray—a healthy wad of spit may work in a pinch—and secure both ends of each grip with thin-gauge wire, available at any hardware store. Tighten the wire down by twisting it around the ends with a pair of pliers. Be sure there are no sharp wire ends sticking out to slice your hands and make you wish you hadn't forgotten your gloves.

CHAPTER 4

Climbing and Shifting

Climbing is the true measure of a rider's strength, endurance, technical sensitivity, and (who can forget?) pain threshold. Closely related to the technique of climbing is the practice of shifting, which any experienced dirt dog will tell you is the real art of off-road cycling.

Effective climbing has a lot to do with a rider's strength-to-weight ratio, which in turn says a lot about lean body mass—in other words, the leaner the better. Obviously it helps to have a high strength-to-weight ratio, but if this is not the case, all is not lost. Good technical skill, feeling the precise moment when a shift is necessary, the ability to keep both wheels straight, and turning to maximize pedal rpms and power count for a lot. Let's take a closer look.

IT'S SIMPLE, YOU EITHER CLIMB SEATED . . .

On steep, rough, rocky, or loose terrain, you will probably need to stay seated. Keep the bike and especially the bars as stable as possible in order to maximize traction and control. The rule is that you should never leave the saddle unless it is absolutely necessary. In our School of Champions camps and clinics we place a premium on developing core strength, which allows us to stay seated, and thus keep our heart rates down. Well-developed core muscles also enable us to delay the onslaught of lactic buildup, which comes when we continuously tax the primary six or so major muscles used in the motor action of pedaling. (See appendix B on weight training.)

Occasionally you will need to stand to get that extra burst of power to bump yourself over the top of a steep climb. Just be sure you are on stable ground when you rise. Make that transition as smoothly and as quickly as possible, then get back in the saddle again.

Steep undulating terrain presents the greatest challenge to the climber. I suggest surging up very steep terrain features, then cruising over the top to recover from the burst. The forward shifting of body weight will help you match your gear shifts with the roll of the trail. While you have more power standing, it also sends your heart rate through the roof and will extract energy you may need later. Again, experience counts: If the transition

It may not be as powerful, but staying seated and riding the nose of the saddle will get you to the top with your feet off the ground.

is rough, on steep and loose terrain you will lose traction and control the moment your butt leaves the seat.

Always climb seated when it's possible. As a grade gradually steepens, you will probably find your body naturally shifting to the rear of the saddle in an attempt to access the big gluteal and hamstring muscles. Shift gears when your momentum and rpms start to drop off. As the hill begins getting uncomfortable, shift your body weight forward, onto the nose of your saddle, to improve your weight distribution and keep the front wheel on the ground. Although this stance shortens your leg extension and robs you of power, the trade-off is worthwhile on the very steep stuff, where leaving the saddle would produce immediate wheel spin and probably necessitate a "dab"—a touch of the ground with your foot. Use your bar-end extensions for added leverage when the going gets steep.

...OR YOU CLIMB STANDING

On short grades with firm but steep and or uneven surfaces, especially when power and speed are factors (e.g., racing), you can generate a lot more leverage (15 to 20 percent) by standing. The side-to-side swinging of the bike that accompanies standing increases body weight through each pedal stroke. Just as with road bikes, when you leave the saddle you may occasionally find it necessary to shift into a slightly higher gear because of the increase in power. Keep your rpms and heart rate as constant as possible.

Remember to time your power stroke (see photo) so the primary driving force is generated from the top of the stroke (from the 12 o'clock position to about 5 o'clock) in a dominant lead-

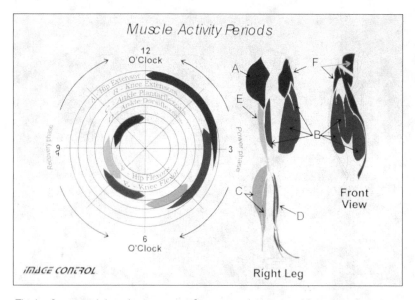

Think of your pedal stroke in terms of power and recovery. Note that the major-ity of your muscle mass is being fired during the power, or 12 to 5 o'clock, portion of your stroke. A clear understanding of the power-and-recovery principle as it relates to muscle firing will improve your coordination and crank timing when ped-aling out of the saddle.

ing-toe position* in order to generate a smooth transition of power through the recovering up-stroke. By contrast, if your force is generated at the top and bottom of the circle, your power will fall off considerably from poor timing. Instead of generating forward momentum, you will find your rhythm out of sync as your body weight is simply driven up into the sky and down into the turf. This is probably the most common mistake beginners make when climbing out of the saddle.

---

* The "leading-toe position" simply means that the toe will be dropped and lead-ing the stroke through the power phase of the pedaling cycle. This is known as plantar flexion, and it actually assists the leg in utilizing more power from the lower leg muscles during the recovery portion of the pedal stroke.

Standing requires a well-timed lean with power driven forward and good stroke mechanics to avoid overpowering and spinning the rear wheel.

The scourge of many beginners: Letting the front wheel swing off-center means an immediate loss of forward momentum on hills. Keep those wheels in line.

Canting on climbs: As you power up steeper, slower grades on rough and especially rocky surfaces you may discover how to protect your rear derailleur, cranks, pedals, chainrings, and even your feet by canting the bike away from obstacles at the bottom of the stroke. Canting can also be used to clear tight trees and branches.

Ratcheting in the rough: Ratcheting is a variation on the same theme used on flats or slight grades. This technique helps you negotiate minefields of natural objects like rocks and branches. It is also a common technique used to keep your feet relatively dry when pedaling through shallow water crossings. Pump your cranks at the 3 and 9 o'clock positions to produce power without making a full revolution of the cranks.

The second most common mistake that most of us make is swinging the front wheel off-center. In other words, the front and rear wheels are crossing each other, which means we are losing momentum. Keep those wheels as aligned as possible as you climb while standing. As with the seated climb, use your bar extensions for more leverage.

GEAR CHANGING

A big part of effective climbing is the coordination of precise shifting with perfectly balanced pedal strokes. Shift your gears before you hit a tough sharp grade. Shifting at the last moment will force you to sweep the range too quickly, and sometimes this results in a thrown or jammed chain at the worst possible time. Keep your rpms constant and time your shift points to be right on. Gear choice depends totally on your range of fitness and strength. If the gear is too low, you'll lose vital power and momentum by overspinning. On the other hand, if the gear beats you up, you'll lose speed and energy by taxing yourself into anaerobic debt before you reach the top of a grade. Practice several different gear choices for a variety of grades until your shifts accurately mimic your body's own energy capabilities.

Anyone who has ever ridden a bike knows the feel of lactic burn caused by oxygen starvation. Choosing optimum gears is a matter of practice and familiarity with the terrain. In the thick of the fight, you should be able to be make correct choices based on feel rather than conscious judgment. Practice sessions over a range of terrains will reduce decision making to pure instinct.

CHAPTER 5

Getting Down

Give me a clear blue sky over my head, and the green turf beneath my feet, a winding road before me, and a three hours' march to dinner.

—William Hazlitt, 1821

ood descending means learning from your mistakes, and the best way to learn is to do.

In the beginning, all novice riders everywhere lock their arms and nail themselves onto their saddles. Instead, adopt a flexible posture in and out of the saddle when descending. Your legs should respond like shock absorbers. Although you shouldn't try to ride with pros from the start, there are great advantages to trying to look like a pro from the very beginning. When I say look like a pro, I'm talking not about speed but about form on the bike, the manner in which you pour your body over the machine.

Most beginners I've introduced to trail riding seem about as comfortable at the sight of their first real downhill as they would be meeting the demon from their worst nightmare. I don't want it to be like that for you. After you have been doing this for a while, you will probably recall your first downhill the way I do, as a rigid experience. Your elbows were probably locked, your hands in a white-knuckled death grip on the handlebars, your teeth clenched, your butt glued to the saddle, and you probably had a look of terror in your eyes.

The most important thing is learning to stay loose and enjoy the ride, the scenery, the fresh air, and the blue sky. You'll remember this experience for the rest of your life. If you've been on the trail before, try to remember being very young. Children are the most natural athletes. With no preconceived notions about anything, and no fears, their play is unconditional. Whether your last bike ride was a decade ago, last year, or even yesterday, it really doesn't matter: The goal is to cover ground, looking at technical obstacles as invitations rather than warnings.

Relax and let your bike become your therapist. Paradoxically, your time as a beginner is when you make your greatest technical gains. Mount up and follow me.

THE DESCENT

If you're like most of us, your first radical off-road sensation will probably come from losing altitude. Find a smooth, steep hill somewhere and spend some time just looking down the slope. Stand there for a moment and take it all in.

Praise this compound machine, conceived by da Vinci and perfected by Shimano. Efficiency experts tell us that a man or woman fueled with oatmeal and riding a bike—let's call it a mountain bike—is the most efficient traveler on the planet. Savor that thought. It makes me feel good knowing that in this age of instant global transportation, when I'm in shape, my bike and I are actually more efficient than any device yet devised to move people.

FORM

Before, during, and after this first descent take stock of your body position. Is your stance relaxed, with bent elbows, or is it unbending and rigid? The former will get you home in one piece; the latter will just pound the living crap out of you. The idea is to minimize the transmission of shock through the muscles and skeletal structure. Simply bending the elbows and riding in a semicrouched position off the saddle will allow you a more balanced distribution of weight. This position will unlock your joints and spine and allow you to use your upper and lower limbs like sophisticated and independent shock absorbers.

Your saddle should be an inch or two lower than normal. This will inspire greater confidence and allow you to easily tap the ground with your foot for balance. Later, as you get comfortable on the bike, you can raise the saddle to leverage more biomechanical force for cross-country. The goal is to find the perfect balance of power and comfort.

A starting-out position means a low center of gravity, with the ground a quick foot tap away.

After finding your own blend of comfort and control on a particular descent, begin doing some low-speed maneuvers. Search for the best line on every trail. Practice getting out of the saddle and getting back in as you descend. Get that weight back and be prepared to go even farther back. Your arms should be extended, but never locked. Locked joints means you have no suspension for your body.

Another big priority is to make sure you are comfortable with your shoe and pedal system. Getting in and out of your

Don't let your pedal system trap you. Get comfortable with entry and exit procedures before you hit the trail.

Carving cones or obstacles in the trail is a good way to get comfortable and get a feel for your bike.

pedals with ease is critical to maintaining balance and control. Effective foot dabbing comes from being able to release on impulse at the first sign of trouble. If you can't get out of the pedal with a quick flick of the ankle, then back in instantaneously, you don't have complete control over your bike. Subtle shifts in body weight are transmitted directly to the ground through the pedals. The relationship of feet to pedals has a great deal to do with effective off-road maneuvering.

On smooth, straight, fast descents (a regular paved road is a perfectly acceptable alternative for beginners) try lowering your head and bending your elbows to get closer to the bars, thus lowering your center of gravity and making the bike more stable. Hold the pedal cranks at the 3 and 9 o'clock positions to improve stability. From this position, come up suddenly and make a parachute out of your body. Feel how body position affects aerodynamics and control. If conditions are safe, try doing some loose serpentine turns to further enhance the feeling of oneness with your bike.

BRAKING ON A DESCENT

As hard as it may seem to grasp, never forget that speed is your ally. That's right: You're actually safer on descents if you stay off the brakes. Brake only when you know you have plenty of traction. On extremely rough surfaces, stay off the brakes and let the blood flow back into your hands. Braking in the rough will transmit more shock into your bike and thus your body, with the end result being a lack of control. As you approach steeper descents balance the pedals at the 3 and 9 o'clock positions, then hold your weight back behind the saddle—way, way back on the steeper descents. Keep your eyes trained forward on the trail in front of you. Cast your eyes in the general area of where you want to be in the next few seconds.

Precise balance is maintained with minor adjustments of the knees. Like a control surface on an airplane, your body weight is trimmed up and down, fore and aft, as needed. The term "body English" best describes adjustments that help dictate line of travel. I have noticed that the real aficionados of downhill have very fluid hips and knees and make killer downhill skiers and dancers. Many control maneuvers start with hip rotation, then progress to arms and shoulders. As you descend, practice keeping your entire body in motion. Remember to breathe deeply through each maneuver. Like the water sloshing around in your water bottle, you should be fluid.

If the descent gets hairy you will need to be spot on with your braking. Activating the rear brake enough to semilock the wheel while giving simultaneous light dabs on the front brake is sometimes the best method for descending. As noted previously, this is called feather braking, and that's exactly what it is. But use a tad too much front braking or a slightly canted front wheel and over the bars you go. When descending steep terrain like this, brake and body control are maintained with a delicate balance that sometimes requires a slow fishtailing. If expedience (e.g., during a race) is your priority, you might pedal down the hill, but the trick is to know your limits. Never wait until the race to try something new; if you have any doubts, opt for safety with a dismount and a run down. I remember one ghoulish bastard in the huge crowd on the Extreme at the 1995 NORBA Nationals at Mammoth Lakes, California, yelling "Front brake! Front brake!" to the racers as they flung themselves

As with any sport, in mountain biking skill comes with patience and practice and a healthy measure of self-confidence.

down the precipitous descent. Sure enough, the idea stuck, and in short order about a dozen bodies were piled up like unstacked cordwood at the bottom of the Extreme.

Learning to keep your hand clear of the front brake handle, maintaining a body position well behind the seat, and making subtle steering adjustments take some time to master. In the next chapter, on cornering, I will discuss steering in more depth. A key element in descending is attitude. Through short and careful practice sessions you will learn to respond to conditions with a sense of calm resolve rather than panic.

CHAPTER 6

Drilling Corners

FLAT TRACKIN'

An experienced road-racing friend recently announced a switch of allegiance to mountain biking and asked me about steering differences in the dirt. I told her to start by forgetting everything she knew about cornering a road bike.

Most of my off-road students come from road backgrounds. The first thing I do is get them to loosen up and let go of all anxiety. The usual procedure is to break them in with a slip 'n' slide routine on an open, preferably flat, section of packed dirt or an unpaved and empty parking lot large enough to execute a series

For the fearless among us, the quickest way to increase technical skills is to hang out with a BMXer of a different generation. Here's Cheri Elliott, BMX Hall of Famer, showing us how it's done.

of geometric configurations. These shapes generally resemble a series of circles and rectangles, all done in rapid succession, like some crazed substitute teacher's idea of kinetic geometry.

The course should incorporate different consistencies of dirt or even sand, with a little gravel thrown in for good measure. The object is to gradually, and I emphasize *gradually*, increase your cornering speed and relax your inhibitions. The way to do this is to take the course slowly at first, and then faster and faster, until you are eventually tracking on the knobbed edges of your tires. I want you to feel the bite of the tires change as they start tracking on the edges. Pay particular attention to the scrub that comes with gradual loss of traction. Search for the telltale edges of slippage, and continually push the limits of traction until you are comfortable drifting first the front tire, then both front and rear, while pedaling through a turn.

If your limits are ready for a push, try this exercise with a friend, preferably from the BMX generation.

A TURN FOR THE BETTER

Okay, you feel comfortable in a drift mode, but let me offer a simple caveat grounded in common sense: Single-track trails and fire roads should never be negotiated with utter abandon, especially if they are unfamiliar. When running a downhill turn on a loose surface, instead of sliding your body weight back in the saddle the way you would on the road, try standing on the pedals in the 3 and 9 o'clock positions with your knees bent. Bob Schultz, a former NORBA national champion with tons of teaching experience on bikes and motorcycles, recommends this method of cornering on sharp bends:

Crouch forward on the pedals with your arms bent, elbows out in an aggressive stance. The idea is to keep the upper body fluid, keep your elbows bent, and be ready to shift your weight back or forward as needed. Unlike cornering on the road, the crouched forward position helps absorb shock. This forward position allows you to make sharper turns faster by literally throwing your body weight into the turn.

Instead of the traditional 6 and 12 o'clock foot positions preferred by fast-banking roadies, Bob suggests adopting the 3 and 9 o'clock pedal positions for improved weight distribution and balance. When executing a turn on loose gravel or soft dirt, set up wide and begin your turn early enough to straighten slightly should you hit some loose stuff. Splay your knee to the inside of the turn and dip your body weight in the direction of the turn to help dictate your line of travel.

When cornering rapidly on a series of downhill turns, timing is critical; should you lose your rhythm on an early set of turns, the error will compound as you go. The best downhillers seem to follow a policy of "into the turn slow, out of the turn fast." Beginners, I have noticed, seem to do just the opposite and then wonder what happened as as they pick themselves up.

A good front- or, better yet, dual-suspension bike will make you faster by allowing you to take the fastest line in a turn or downhill instead of always searching for the one your mother would want you to pick. A word of caution, however: Don't let that super equipment boost your confidence beyond your technical abilities. The key is to raise your requisite skill level slowly before you go bonkers.

Sometimes cornering on dirt requires less steering input and more weight transfer. As the turn deepens, drop the inside knee and maybe the elbow in the direction of the turn.

An effective technique popularized by pro racer John Tomac is this footloose method of maintaining balance while sliding through a turn. The purpose of the dangling inside leg has less to do with stopping a too-far slide and more to do with altered weight distribution, which facilitates a speedy entry and departure. Even so, if you've leaned too far, you can easily correct it with a quick dab of the foot.

Compare and contrast the cross-country style with Dave Cullinan's more upright and stable downhill and slalom position.

SLALOM RUNNIN'

If you come from a skiing background, the transition to MTBing is going to seem as familiar as peanut butter and jelly. In slalom running, you are essentially cutting a series of linked S-turns on the trail. Just as you weight and unweight your turns in snow, so you will do on dirt. As you set up for the turn and begin changing your line, unweight the wheels by sitting up and straightening your arms. Your weight is neutralized and the G-force is minimized, allowing for a smoother arc on the turn. As you proceed past the apex, or midpoint, of the turn and need greater traction, drive your force down to maximize loading of the front tire. Transfer your weight forward slightly, with your arms bent. Shift your hips forward—in total contrast to the back-in-the-saddle form used in road racing.

NORBA national slalom champ Cheri Elliott shows us how to run a slalom.

OFF-CAMBER TURNS

Obviously, not all turns are flat. On an off-camber turn, leaning the bike into the turn and counterleaning the body in the opposite direction is usually your safest procedure. A close look at most NORBA races will reveal that many top riders choose

Sometimes counterleaning is a more comfortable method of getting down and around. Counterleaning is an especially effective method of cornering on a reverse camber, as illustrated here.

this approach, because it improves traction. Negotiating banks that flow away from you requires the utmost concentration. Instead of the usual wide approach with a tight squeeze of the apex, as described earlier by Schultz, you need to lean the bike into the bank and counterbalance by tilting your body weight in the opposite direction.

CORNERING IN MUD

A muddy corner is difficult enough, but typically such corners are also off-camber. In wet weather, race courses tend to deteriorate pretty quickly, and just when you think things can't get any worse, a slippery tree root suddenly exposes itself across the trail. (East Coast courses are notorious for these conditions.) Under such circumstances, reducing your speed to a crawl by feathering both brakes and keeping the bike as upright as possible with a wide arcing turn are givens. Your next order of business is to get the inside foot out to lower your center of gravity, which helps compensate for the reversed camber.

Just before the point of impact with the root, slide your weight back in the saddle slightly and straighten your line to keep the bike upright. The weight from your outstretched leg will both serve as a balance point as the corner becomes slick and as a pivot to turn your body and bike around, in the direction of the turn, when the surface gets really treacherous. This is accomplished by lifting the handlebars as the foot strikes the turf. After you are through the turn, a skateboard shove with the downed foot, or a pull off a tree branch, might just be the ticket for getting back your momentum when rear-wheel traction is at a minimum.

STEERED AND UNSTEERED TURNS

One of my favorite teaching techniques is the practice of steered and unsteered turning. In broad strokes, there are two types of turns: those executed primarily from controlling the handlebars —steered, and those generated mainly by the adjustment of body weight with little actual steering input—unsteered. The steered turns are used for much tighter execution, something like a tight, technical section of a single track, for example. Unsteered turns require subtle weight transfer; usually a knee and an elbow are dropped in the direction of the turn, as previously described. This method is used for wide, sweeping turns and is generally considered the safest way to negotiate a high-speed turn.

Of course, there will be variations on the theme of steered and unsteered turning. Some turns will require a little of both. Save yourself some skin by practicing a combination of them. I recommend finding some fellow riders and a challenging down-hill course. Grab a few pylons. (Gallon milk containers with a bit of sand in them to prevent drift will work fine.) Starting with the pylons close together, do a series of short, low-speed steered turns. After a few runs between the pylons, you will find your timing and coordination improving. As with any skill, your cornering techniques will improve with relaxed reinforcement. Remember, start slow and pay attention to your technique. As with skiing, speed and efficiency will come with experience.

When you feel comfortable with the slow-speed maneuver-ing, try some faster play with the pylons set farther apart. This time try cornering in a slightly more aggressive manner.

The last phase of this exercise is usually the most fun. It involves some friendly competition. By now I'm assuming you've overcome most of your cornering anxiety, in which case it's time to bring out a stopwatch. I find that the introduction of a low-key element of competition accelerates the learning curve. I set up organized technical practice sessions and frequently introduce new courses to constantly challenge participants.

Cornering without the benefit of practice can leave you behind—or on your behind—depending on the saving grace of your experience. With skill and a good prerun, you can push your own limits safely with greater speed than you ever imagined possible in your other life.

CHAPTER 7

Jump Wisdom

ONE WHEEL UP . . .

About the time you start feeling comfortable and grounded, it's time to leave earth behind. Executing a smooth jump should start on flat ground. Begin by simply sliding your weight back in the saddle. Practice this maneuver until it is smooth. As you move back in the saddle, set your cranks at the horizontal 3 and 9. As your weight comes back, gently lift the handlebars until the front wheel leaves the ground. Begin by lifting the bike over nothing at all, then gradually progress from a small twig to a piece of lumber, each time increasing the size of the object. Once you are comfortable with this progression, start looking for low curbs and work your way right up to small buildings.

Remember, the method for jumping low curbs is the same as for high curbs and logs.

Here are some basic steps for lifting:

1. Slide back in the saddle.
2. Pull up on your bars and gently lift the front wheel.
3. After your front wheel has cleared the object, transfer your weight slightly forward, using this forward momentum to pop the rear wheel up and over.
4. Finally, redistribute your weight back over the rear wheel for stability.

Ponder each phase of this maneuver slowly in your mind, then put those thoughts into action. Make sure you have enough forward momentum to execute the sequence as a single, smooth maneuver. Spend as much time as you need on developing each phase of this hop. Hopping is a fundamental skill that needs to be mastered sooner rather than later.

Getting over an object like a log requires several simultaneous movements. First, slide back in the saddle and pull up on the bars.

The front wheel comes up and the rear wheel follows up and over.

Last, transfer weight back over the rear wheel for stability.

For the more experienced rider who has mastered the three-step manuever of clearing the log, Dave Cullinan demonstrates clearing the log with a single ballistic hop.

CATCHING A LITTLE AIR

The old motorcycle axiom "When your wheels are off the ground, you're not racing" is especially true in mountain biking, where you'll usually pay dearly for that extra air with an elevated heart rate. But having said that, let's look at flying in a different way: It's cool to fly. Not only that, aerial maneuvering is one of mountain biking's tricks that will add to your technical repertoire and quotient of fun. Besides, who's racing? Sometimes it's actually safer to fly over, or "clean" (mountainbike parlance for "clear"), an object or rut that would otherwise trip you if you were to swallow it with full impact.

In executing a two-wheel jump, practice the same barlifting motion you used in the single-wheel jump. The difference is that this time you're going to approach with a bit more gusto. The cranks are preset horizontally at 3 and 9 and the body is coiled off the seat in balanced preparation for the leap. This time, the tug on the bars has two purposes:

- To add momentum to your loft.
- To locate your balance point.

Hold the bars in a semirelaxed but firm grip—not a death grip. Get into the habit of bending your knees in an up-and-down bouncing mode—imagine you're on a pogo stick. This will facilitate the full "spring" motion to follow. The trick to effective jumping is to find the perfect body-balance point that allows you to lift both wheels together. Practice this maneuver by building some speed, coiling and jumping, then coiling and jumping again several times until you can leave the ground with both wheels equally balanced and return them to the ground in the same manner. It's important to have your timing and carrying speed just right as you near the jump.

It's also important to get your body weight back to make the bike land on the infinitely more stable rear wheel instead of the front. Shifting your body weight to change your landing will further increase your level of confidence. Smooth two-wheeled landings are another priority in bike piloting.

A series of downhill driveway ramps or a particular sloping berm on your favorite trail may provide the perfect feature for practicing and nailing this stuff down. Once you get the hang of of the technique, you can start working on higher jumps.

For you trail hounds and BMXers who are ho-humming this basic stuff, let me lead you through a trail condition we discovered while shooting these photos with former world champion Dave Cullinan.

Our downhill trail rose very suddenly, with a large water bar across the trail, giving Dave the potential for some fairly serious loft. The challenge came the next few feet down, where the trail broke sharply to the left. Dave nailed the water bar with just enough carrying speed from the jump to get airborne for a long second or so, with his elbows bent in anticipation of a smooth landing. In the next millisecond he adjusted his hips slightly to the right and at the same time rotated the bars and the front wheel in midair. The centrifugal force of the spinning wheel redirected the entire bike to the left, thus kicking the rear wheel out slightly to the right and canting the bike to the left in the direction of the trail jog. In the next tick of the clock, he was entering the landing zone, which was strewn with small, loose granite rocks. His intuitive response was to center his body to make sure both wheels landed at the same time. Just

The high-flying former world champion Dave Cullinan demonstrates his flawless technique, sure to bring a few high fives.

before touching down, he delicately straightened his body, with both wheels aligned, and adjusted to the new direction of travel. Sound familiar?

ABSORBING BUMPS

What goes up must come down. It's a fact that our bodies are many times more efficient than even the latest high-tech suspension systems. Remember the oatmeal example? Such facts seem to make traversing rough country and downhills a little easier. Imagine yourself running flat-out down a semitechnical trail with a series of obstacles. Focus your attention on the general layout of the terrain. Avoid fixations with immediate objects—we tend to take aim at things that catch our gaze, like bumps and rocks. Instead, cast your eyes to the broader layout of the trail as it unfolds in front of you.

As you rise from the earth, bend your elbows and raise your body to a more upright and slightly forward position to allow your body to absorb what your bike's suspension doesn't. Avoid stiffening your muscles in anticipation of the bike absorbing the landing; instead, keep your body loose and share the impact. If you are desending a rapid downhill and catch air on a rise, let the bike drift while you relax and set the front wheel, your head, and the core of your body weight in a clearly downhill direction for touchdown.

Practice connecting your series of moves like a written signature. Each move is like a letter, dependent on the one just before and the one just after. Hold the grips as you would a paintbrush, with a light, fluid grip. If your grip is too tight, all the muscles from the trapeziuses to the flexors and extensors of the wrists, hands, and fingers will tighten and quickly tire, making braking and control more difficult. After each technical run, stop and consider the interconnected moves you just made and replay the images you liked.

Descending in the semicrouched "ready" position, your body should feel light, your elbows bent in anticipation of the terrain. Your weight should be on the pedals. Let your lower body and bike suspension absorb the ups and downs of a particular course. In the process, divert your eyes to the next set of conditions, with your body's movements slightly ahead of the bike's movements. You are turning your body into a sponge.

For maximum integration of these technical skills, it is far better to allow yourself a few short sessions daily than a long continuous practice time. Do your technical training at the beginning of the ride, when you're fresh, rather than at the end. Once again, treat this stuff as play, and your mind and body will snap the pieces together as systematically as you would a jigsaw puzzle.

CHAPTER 8

Surviving
the Crash

It can happen to you, then it can happen again.
　　　　　　　　—Steve McQueen, in the movie *Le Mans*

When the triathlete and mountain biker Scott Tinley came to me to ask for a few appropriate thoughts on biking for his triathlon book some years ago, I gave him a half-serious no-brainer that has followed me so closely I'm quite sure it will end up on my tombstone. Just remember, I said, "There are only two kinds of riders: those who have crashed, and those who are waiting to crash."

Okay, okay, it can happen, it did happen, so what? If you've crash-proofed your body, it's no big deal. One other thing you can do while riding aggressively and taking chances is to be aware of a few "high-frequency" crash situations and avoid them. Beyond that, your only other safeguards are to learn to fall with grace and to always, always wear your helmet and gloves.

Whether you count yourself in the former group or the latter, the fear of falling should be the last reason you have for not riding. Of course, you need to prepare your body by strengthening it for the rigors of the inevitable. In the area of preventive maintenance, I consider strength training a vital ingredient in the process of forestalling injuries to the musculoskeletal

As a beginner or intermediate, one of the first seeds you should plant in your mind is the principle of keeping your pedals level on turns. Even with higher-clearance bottom brackets on mountain bikes, dropping an inside pedal on your turning side can bring you to your knees.

Potentially the most serious of the three common crash ouches is the classic over-the-bars header. This crash scenario occurs for a variety of "over-your-head" reasons. Topping the list would be an excess of weight and momentum forward of the pedal axis. You hit a hole, dip, or rock or maybe miscalculate the height of a rock or log jump, bottom out your front shock, and over you go. Prevention usually means quicker defensive responses, like sliding back in the saddle a tad more quickly in order to place as much weight as possible behind the seat. If the move was so radical that you still did an endo, despite your defensive response, you may have to simply slow down. If you slow down and still end up over the bars, take heart—I've seen some of the most skillful mountain-bike technicians accomplish the same thing. If your loft and load are balanced, aim to vault the bars and do an artful dismount. With luck you should hit the trail running.

system. I recommend both a toughening of anatomy, in a gym, and a user-friendly stretching program to maintain range of motion and flexibility. Strengthening is especially important for downhillers, but we all need the crash-stable security of a tight, hard body. My recommended programs for stretching and strengthening can be found in appendices A and B.

When it comes to crashing, you need to develop an unspoken attitude. Try not to treat crashes as stupid mistakes. Instead, view them as the highest form of learning experience. The process of dialing in, or getting comfortable with a mountain bike, involves a strong element of adventure. When you fall, unless you're just plain unlucky and actually break something, get back up. Instead of taking your toys and going home, take them back up the hill and methodically try it again. Reconstruct the accident and figure out where you screwed up. In your mind correct the procedure and then, on the next run, make it physical. Reinforce the correct technique and line, then quickly move on, being careful not to dwell on past screwups. Re-enacting the mishap and rebuilding your confidence on the spot is a vital exercise in mental toughness and self-preservation.

BAILING OUT

This is going to sound like a broken record, but the most important aspect of abandoning ship is your ability to release quickly from those pedals. I've said it already, but the fact remains: If, after a sufficient break-in period, you can't instantly release from your clips or clipless system, consider giving the pedals to someone you don't like and finding a pair that allow you immediate departure.

It ain't pretty, but the over-the-back bail may well save your head and heart for another day.

Conditions that dictate a bail are usually radically steep downgrades, excessively loose turf, a mechanical failure, or a combination of all of the above. If you find your personal safety compromised by trail conditions that are beyond your ken, get your bum way back over the saddle, pull both feet clear of the pedals, spread your legs, and jump straight back. Your feet should end up just behind the bike with the back wheel between your legs. Use your hands to push the bike forward underneath you, and grab the saddle before it gets away from you.

Sometimes in a make-or-break situation you may need to lay your bike down to avoid smashing into some fixed or otherwise imposing object. This time it's a delivery van in which the driver misjudges your speed and, like a fool, pulls directly across your path with no more warning than an unannounced audit. If you don't have enough time for our previously discussed hot stop, you might just have enough space to nail the rear brake and lay the bike over, sliding into (not under) the vehicle, and thus avoid a full-impact crash. (See chapter 3 on braking.)

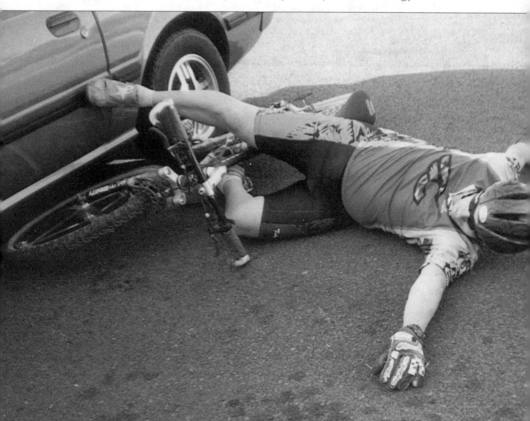

DISMOUNTING ON THE RUN

This technique is primarily used in races to minimize the portage over some unridable object. Even if you have no interest in competing, dismounting on the run is still a useful technique for crossing streams and downed trees, and you can even use the bike to fend off a hungry mountain lion.

The most important consideration for dismounting has to do with timing. In most situations involving portage over unridable objects, such as downed trees, gulleys, and rocks, the best approach is to stay on the bike as long as possible. Don Myrah, one of the United States' best and most consistent cyclo-cross riders, recommends swinging your right leg back over the rear wheel, then forward between you and the frame, just in front of your left leg. At the same time he moves his right hand from the handlebar and grasps the top tube. On dismounting, your left foot should be coming out of the pedal, landing just after the leading right foot. At the same time, pull the bike up with your right hand as you prepare to clear the barrier. An alternative to this that

This series shows the author's slight variation on Don Myrah's technique, with optional tongue action.

works well on longer, steeper climbs is to grab the down tube and hoist the bike straight onto your shoulder.

On the moving remount, the key is to swing the leg over and hit the saddle with the inside of the right thigh—guys will understand this—then roll onto the saddle. Any other method may prove painful.

On a downhill dismount, Myrah recommends getting your body weight back and executing the dismount farther from the actual point of touchdown. In such conditions I find you can actually save energy by coasting up to the obstacle and bracing the right foot on the bottom bracket while riding sidesaddle.

A dismount practice session should start with a snail's-pace walk-through. Emphasize form and balance. Again, spend a good deal of time practicing your pedal exit and entry. Clipless pedals are by far the best choice for this maneuver. Be absolutely certain your tension setting is light enough (taking into consideration conditions such as mud in the cleats) that you can easily twist out before the opposite foot strikes the ground.

IT'S NOT A CRIME TO SKATEBOARD

As the name implies, this technique involves kicking the ground while traversing a steep or rough descent or, as previously described, using your foot to pivot around a very slippery turn. Skateboarding is used when the terrain is too dificult to simply let the bike go. You will want to stay in the saddle and stabilize your position by dabbing the ground with one leg out. During the descent, keep both hands on the brakes, with the usual caution applied to the front.

Skateboarding is not a crime, and neither is getting to the bottom in one piece.

OFF-ROAD RASH

Experienced riders will tell you that a bike and—especially in the case of a mountain bike—its rider are not really broken in until the first crash. Here to offer his advice on dealing with the inevitable consequences of trail rash is Dr. Arnie Baker, author of *Smart Cycling* (Simon & Schuster) and *Bicycling Medicine* (Argo Publishing. Revised edition: Simon & Schuster, 1998).

Off-road rash, the most common bicycling injury, can be treated in different ways. The right way reduces healing time and scarring and allows you to return to your bike promptly.

PREVENTION: Learn bike-handling skills to help prevent falling. Ride defensively, especially in areas that are unfamilar to you. Always wear a helmet.

TREATMENT OBJECTIVES: The objective of treatment is to heal the tissues as rapidly and effectively as possible. Goals of therapy include preventing further damage to the skin and not allowing the depth of the rash to increase in severity.

WHAT CAN GO WRONG? The rash can heal with scarring. The rash can take longer to heal than needed—for example, because of infection. Or the rash can be more painful than necessary during the healing process.

GRADING DIRT RASH: The severity levels of dirt rash are similar to those of burns. A rash can be:

- First degree—only the surface is reddened. This problem does not require active treatment.
- Second degree—the surface layer of the skin is broken, but a deep layer remains that will allow the skin to replace itself and heal without significant scarring.

- Third degree—the skin is entirely removed, perhaps with underlying layers of fat and other supporting tissue strutures exposed. Such damage may require skin grafting and is beyond the scope of this material.

OLD-STYLE TREATMENT: There are two general methods for treatment of second-degree dirt rash. The first is the traditional "let nature take its course" approach. Also called the "open method," this involves cleaning the wound with soap and water, hydrogen peroxide, iodine, or something similar, and then allowing the wound to dry out, form a scab, and "heal on its own."

This method does have its drawbacks for all but the most superficial and small road rashes. Just because you clean it once doesn't mean it won't get infected, especially if the wound is covered with dirt. Bacteria thrive on damaged skin. Infection can increase the depth of the rash, meaning that scarring and delayed healing are more likely. Scabs can crack and become painful. Scabbed areas don't receive oxygen well from the surrounding air, and so take much longer to heal.

MODERN THINKING: The alternative is the "closed approach," in which frequent cleansings and the application of topical antibiotics and dressings keep the rash moist and closed to the air. The area is cleansed at least daily with wet compresses or bathing. Superficial debris is gently removed. An effort is made to remove soft-forming exudates (the beginnings of scabs) with gentle scrubbing. Pink, healthy, new-forming skin is what you want to see.

MODERN-DAY SUPPLIES: Silver sulfadiazine (Silvadene), Polysporin, or mupirocin (Bactroban) is applied. Over the ointment will be layered a Vaseline gauze (e.g., Adaptic), a nonstick mesh that allows removal of the dressing without sticking. Padding in the form of gauze squares may be applied. Then a conforming gauze roll is wrapped around the area and taped in place. Finally, a tube stretch gauze (e.g., Tubigauze) is applied to keep everything in place and tidy.

Alternatively, Tegaderm (3M) or Bioclusive (Johnson & Johnson) alone may be stretched over the antibiotic.

The result is a dressing that allows maximum protection of the wound, minimum risk of infection, prevention of scabbing and its attendant cracking and pain, and healing as fast as possible.

SIDE EFFECTS: Those persons allergic to sulfa drugs should avoid sulfadiazine. Mupirocin is a little better at controlling skin infections, but it's more expensive. Polysporin, available over the counter, is much less likely to irritate the skin than Neosporin.

WATCH FOR SUNBURN ON OFF-ROAD RASH: As the skin nears complete healing, you may be tempted to allow your technique to become lax. Sun exposure, however, may cause the skin to remain permanently darkened after healing, so be sure to keep your rash covered until it's completely healed. Use sunscreen with an SPF greater than 18.

CHAPTER 9

Maintenance

We cyclists can divide ourselves into two categories: techies and nontechies. Those among us who are mechanically oriented tend to be obsessive about details. Ask us mechanical questions—no matter how esoteric—and we will have the answers.

For the rest of us carefree bikies who would rather ride our bikes than work on them, I promise not to make this too painful. In fact, in order to reduce key maintenance items to the bare essentials, I have asked our School of Champions technical consultant, Gerry Rahill, to give us a checklist of basic tune-up reminders. After you digest this information, I suggest you copy it and tape it to the toolbox or refrigerator for future reference. The larger point here is to get you into the habit of checking things and fixing or replacing components before they break and strand you in the middle of no-man's-land.

Even if your maintenance is done by a shop, get into the habit of spot-checking your own bike and diagnosing problems in advance of breakdowns. Get into the habit of doing a check for basics before every ride. Pay particular attention to tire pressure and headset adjustment, new sounds from your chain or cassette, and loose items—cranks and spokes head the list. In stage racing, bikes are used and abused daily until things eventually break. Most experienced racers can share stories with you about how some part or some lack of adjustment cost them a particular race. So here is Gerry's technical advice on simple maintenance and emergency repair. Remember to always carry enough tools to get you home in case something does go wrong.

For the vast majority of us who don't have our own mechanic, we have no one but ourselves to blame if something breaks. If you and your bike travel by air, it is especially important to make sure that the bike arrives undamaged and that you are able to properly reassemble it. It's helpful to investigate local maintenance-friendly bike shops to facilitate reassembly or an emergency replacement if something does end up bent or broken. Cultivating a favorite bike shop should be a priority for all of us. If the range of maintenance described in this chapter is beyond your ken or outside your time frame, I suggest befriending a qualified mechanic at a reputable bike shop. The ideal arrangement is to find a mechanic who can teach you how to fix your own equipment and which tools you'll need. You may not have time to be your own "wrench," but at least you will be able to make emergency repairs when no one else is around.

To help you organize your priorities and consider possible upgrades, Gerry has divided his maintenance checklist into three categories—*safety, performance,* and *prerace.*

Every professional knows that a proper maintenance session should start with a clean bike. Pattern yourself after the team mechanic, who comes to a stage race equipped with a bucket, several sponges, and a supply of brushes ranging from a large stiff-bristled paintbrush to a small toothbrush. Most mechanics use nonabrasive cleansing agents, such as auto paint cleaners, for the actual wash. Avoid solvents and heavy cleaners designed for auto engine degreasing. The problem with these miracle cleaners is that they often break down or wash out essential bearing grease. Scrub and brush all the dirt and grit off the bike. Be thorough, turn it upside down, and get to the bottom of the tubes and components. This is also a good time to clean the chain. Dry it off before starting the maintenance check. Make sure you have all your tools handy, along with your favorite lubricant, several rags, and an old toothbrush.

Always work in well-lighted conditions so you can inspect the frame and components for cracks, bends, rust, looseness, and excessive wear. Look for adjustment problems and make a note of lubrication needs. Your first priority is to perform a safety check to prevent mechanical failure that could cause injury.

Finally, to ensure your bike is running at top efficiency, conduct the performance check.

Good mechanics on the NORBA circuit are frequently the most popular people at the races. The reason is simple: Things are always breaking.

SAFETY CHECK

ITEM	REGULAR MAINTENANCE
Frame	There should be no cracks or separation in tubes or lugs, or bent or dented tubes. Check rear triangle (make sure derailleur hanger and tips and drops are straight). Touch up scratches—sand and prime to avoid rust. Check for proper alignment: Can you ride with no hands and have the bike maintain a straight line? Does the rear wheel slide in and out freely?
(Tools:	*Actual frame alignment is best left up to your favorite pro shop.)*
Headset	Check for smooth operation and looseness.
(Tools:	*Expander bolt system—two multipurpose headset wrenches and Allen key. A-head type system—single 5mm Allen key.)*
Bars and stem	Make sure they're tight.
(Tools:	*Allen key.)*
Hand grips	Make sure they're tight.
Brake levers	Make sure they're secured snugly and that the adjustment prevents them from "bottoming out" against bars.
(Tools:	*Depending on type of brake: Allen key, socket wrench, or screwdriver.)*
Brakes	Make sure there are no worn pads or frayed or rusty cables and that mounting bolts are tight. Lube pivots and springs.
(Tools:	*Allen key or box-end wrench, "third-hand" tool.)*
Seat post:	Make sure the seat post is tight and the seat has no tilt or side-to-side twist.
(Tools:	*Allen key or box-end wrench. Always travel with an extra seat-post binder bolt.)*
Gears	Make sure there are no frayed or rusty cables. Check high- and low-gear adjustment stops. Lube pivots. Check indexing by sweeping the range from bottom to top and back on both front and rear shifters.
(Tools:	*Small regular or Phillips-head screwdriver, Allen keys.)*

SAFETY CHECK (CONT.)

Wheels and rims Make sure there are no cracks in rims around spoke holes or on sides and no big dents or bulges that could affect safe braking.

(Tools: Spoke wrench, cone wrenches.)

Bottom bracket Check for no play in adjustable units and smooth operation in sealed brackets.

(Tools: Bottom bracket wrenches for lock ring and adjustable cups. Up-to-date sealed units require only an installation tool.)

Chain Chain should have no stiff links or heavy buildup of grime and should be well lubed.
Double-check new chains for stiff links before hitting the trail. (Work the links with your fingers until they move freely.)

(Tools: Chain rivet extractor.)

Tires Although the trend seems headed in the direction of the faster sparse-tread Ritchey SpeedMax design for dry conditions, make sure you have plenty of tread left for steep climbs and muck running. (Check sidewalls for broken cords, cuts in tread.)

(Tools: Tire gauge, tire irons [levers], workable hand pump and/or CO_2 cartridges for competition.)

Pedals Clips and straps should not be cracked, broken, or excessively worn.
Pedals should be threaded tightly into cranks.
Clipless pedals should release quickly, smoothly, and effortlessly.

(Tools: Pedal wrench or open-end adjustable wrench, or manufacturer's assembly tools.)

Cassette and freewheel cogs Replace any cogs that show worn or broken teeth or that skip after replacing the chain.

(Tools: Chain whip and freewheel remover; use your favorite lubrication based on operating conditions.)

Crank arms Check for cracks and bends.
Crank bolts and chainring bolts should be tight.

(Tools: Two-part crank-removal tools; spanner and threaded internal remover if required.)

PERFORMANCE CHECK

Frame	Should have perfect alignment—a job for a well-equipped shop specializing in frame alignment.
Headset	Should turn freely and not be worn or "indexed."
Bars and stem	Check for tight connection.
Hand grips	Should have no movement and should be secured with wire or glue to prevent moisture contamination and movement.
Brake levers	Correct adjustment for hard braking under given conditions.
Brakes	Should have daylight between all pads and rims. Check for cracks or bends in housing. "Toe in" pads to eliminate squeaking.
Seat post	Recheck position based on body mechanics and course conditions. (See chapter 2 on correct positioning.)
Gears	Lube cables. Don't forget under the bottom bracket. Check limit screw adjustments and indexing.
Wheels	Should be true, round, and dished with spokes properly tensioned.
Bottom bracket	For nonsealed units, make sure bearings and cups are adjusted smoothly and the unit is well greased. There should be no lateral movement in bottom bracket. For sealed units, telltale squeaking or looseness indicates imminent failure.
Chain	Lube, if dry. Replace, if worn. Measure the old chain from pin to pin. If it's more than an $\frac{1}{8}$" longer than a new chain, it needs to be replaced to prevent excessive wear to the cassette and chainrings.
Tires	Inflate to correct pressure as determined by conditions and prior experience.
Pedals	Check that bearings perform smoothly. Replace worn or damaged cleats.

PERFORMANCE CHECK (CONT.)

Cassette and freewheel cogs	Replace worn cogs. Lube freewheel bearings, if necessary.
Chainrings	Replace rings if excessively worn (teeth broken off) or twisted. Straighten if bent.
Emergency tools	Pump, chain breaker, spoke wrench (know how to use it), tire irons, spare tube, full patch kit and material for a tire boot, various Allen wrenches, a good working pump, change for a phone call. Optional: CO_2 activator and cartridges.
Special note:	*I am assuming you know how to use all of the above emergency items and can quickly repair the bike in the event of trouble.*

PRERACE CHECK

Wheels Check that rims run true with no dings, that hubs are smooth, that tires are free of thorns, etc., that nipples are not rounded, and that there are no cracks in rim near eyelets.

Shocks Check that air and oil shock seals are not leaking oil, that sliders are free of dirt and dust, that there are no dings in sliders or stanchions, and that fork brace is tight.

Headset Check that it turns smoothly with no scoring or play and that lock ring is tight.

Bottom bracket Check that bottom bracket runs smoothly with no binding or wobble.

Cranks Check that crank bolts are tight, with no creaking.

Chainrings Bolts should be on tight, rims straight, teeth not missing or worn.

Pedals Should be on tight, bearings well lubed; if clipless, should be free of dirt.

Chain Check for wear, rust, and stiff links. Should be well lubed.

Cogs Should have no broken or worn teeth; remove all dirt and grime.

Bars and stem Should be tight and should not creak.

Grips Grips should not be torn or slide. Install tie wraps or wire (see earlier description on page 42).

Shifters Check that cables are not frayed or rusting and that housing not bent or cracked.

Derailleurs Pulley wheels should be tight but not binding. Anchor bolts should be tight. Front derailleur should be at correct height and alignment, and should have correct indexing—both front and rear.

Brakes All cables should be capped. Check housing for dents and cracks. Brake arms should move freely and shoes grip rims evenly. Check all fixing bolts for security.

CHAPTER 10

The Ten Commandments of Single Track

(with Apologies to Moses)

Thou shalt . . .

1.

. . . turn this fat-tired vehicle into an escape mechanism from the urban jungle and the principles of internal combustion. Not only is this steed a physical extension of body, it is a roaring expression of your limitlessness.

2.

. . . get comfortable with your shoe and pedal combination. It's important to avoid those stupid slow-speed tip-overs. You should be able to click in and out with such rapidity and ease that such action draws admiring glances from your riding partners.

3.

. . . learn to speak body language and pay attention to balance and weight distribution. Don't glue yourself to the saddle as if riding the pave'.

4.

. . . start by slip-sliding around a gravel or dirt oval. Learn to feel comfortable in "mode le drift." Such progressive breaks with the well-grounded world of traction will accustom you to the limits of both tires and nerves.

5.

. . . descend and learn to swallow bumps by staying loose. Keep your butt off the saddle, with your elbows bent, and rock the bike back and forth as terrain requires.

6.

. . . ride on a variety of trail conditions, not just single tracks, to learn to feel the subtle differences created by varying tire pressure. Measure improvement in terms of comfort and control.

7.

. . . praise rainstorms and treat them not only as a renewal of the life cycle but also as another opportunity to gain valuable practice time even though it may cause grief to your significant other.

8.

. . . learn to jump things by coiling your body and lifting the front wheel, then pulling forward and letting the rear follow. Start by leaping nothing but your shadow and progress to berms, logs, and small curbed autos.

9.

. . . shred lightly and be a responsible citizen. Be kind to the trail and understanding of necessary trail closures. Avoid sensitive areas, especially in the early spring, and above all respect the rights of hikers and horsefolk.

10.

. . . always take care to pay your personal health-insurance premiums on time; then remember it is impossible to put a price on sheer shit-faced fun.

CHAPTER 11

Racing
on the Mind

Don't worry about getting rid of the butterflies, just get them to fly in formation.

THE PRERUN

If you are planning to do a race, take the time to prerun the course before riding it at speed. If you are unfamiliar with the course, come in early and check it out—either on foot or by riding it. The off-road prerun is vital for preparing for the real thing. In a prerun, you establish your brake and shift points and correct lines of entry and exit. I've followed top experts and pros through tricky downhill turns only to see them stop, turn around, and go back up the hill to run the course again; they'll even walk a tricky section, in order to read the terrain and memorize it.

Factors to consider include surface conditions on race day, camber adjustment of each turn, and the bank of a berm—sometimes it's favorable, sometimes not. Occasionally there is moisture, sand, or extra-loose debris. If you are racing in the afternoon and the only time you could do a prerun was morning, go back down and walk the course again just before you race. The little knoll you used for big air in practice may be a dangerous eight-inch-deep hole by afternoon. The same is true of a cross-country course, so always cruise your first lap and take mental pictures.

RACE STARTS

National and world champion Ned Overend believes that getting off the line is vital to the outcome of a race. Ned makes a point of choosing the right gear before the start of an event.

More often than not, races start very fast, especially if there is a section of single track coming up. I recommend never going completely anaerobic—also known as entering lactic hell—at the start of any event. Just as if you were riding a road race, pick a fast and smooth wheel to sit on and constantly put yourself in a position to move up, through, or around the pack. By all means make your move on a field before you get to a single-track section. Once ensconced in good position on a single track, you can cruise, but if you lose a lot of ground before hitting that section, you may never see the leaders until the awards ceremony.

SPECIALTY EQUIPMENT

Dual-Slalom Bikes. This specialty mountain-bike competition borrowed its name from skiing. Just as with skiing, the racers line up for what amounts to a gated, zig-and-zag drag race to the bottom. Dual-slalom bikes are fairly useless animals for anything but zigging and zagging. These machines resemble mutant BMXs with gears. Frames are notably smaller than those used for cross-country. The bike seats are usually low—real low—so the riders can maintain a low center of gravity when carving. The seats are also tipped up slightly to facilitate up-and-down movement—not that they see much use, since most slalom riders spend the short burst in suspension and out of the saddle. Because of the tremendous slamming these machines take, you will always find a chain tensioner on duty.

Downhill Bikes. Also borrowing a name from skiing, downhilling is as simple as taking the ski lift up and going down. What is not so simple is the equipment. Downhilling has provided bike engineers with plenty of challenging problems to solve in the quest for better equipment on specific courses. Bikes are changing so fast that even periodicals are hard pressed to keep up with the latest technological advances. Downhill bikes are the Formula Ones of bike racing. They represent the lion's share of any factory racing budget. Virtually all downhill bikes are equipped with dual suspension, and they are often referred to as "soft-tails."

FORKS AND SUSPENSIONS: Extra-long travel forks and dual suspensions with just enough rigidity to withstand high-speed descents are the ticket. Gone are the elastomers in the front, and springs have replaced air in the rear.

BRAKES: Critical for downhilling. Braking late and sprinting out of turns require foolproof, no-fade clamping power, the kind of power you get from discs that produce virtually no frame flex, heat buildup, or fade. Sure-gripping hydraulics are also seen on a few downhill rigs these days.

PEDALS: Downhillers, who are continually in and out of their pedals, prefer the older, wider Shimano M737 pedals over the smaller, lighter-bodied cross-country pedals.

TIRES: Tires should have plenty of width and good stiff side-knobs that allow for lots of slip-sliding directional variation.

SEAT HEIGHT: Racers typically position their saddles quite a bit lower than cross-country riders, trading power for stability with a lower center of gravity.

GEARS: With the higher speeds of downhilling comes the need for larger chainrings. (Sixty or more teeth are common on the fastest downhill courses, such as the infamous Kamikaze at Mammoth. On the average cross-country bike, the teeth on the large chainring number in the forties.) Like the slalom machines, downhill bikes have chain tensioners to keep the drivetrain driving under extreme conditions.

In this specialist's world, it is nearly impossible for a racer to be multidisciplinary and excel in different races using only a single bike anymore, although this does not preclude many of us from competing in downhill on our cross-country bikes for the sheer thrill of self-exploration.

Cross-Country Bikes. As the name implies, this is the endurance phase of mountain-bike racing. Races usually traverse ski runs and frequently include two or three thousand vertical feet of climbing in a two-hour race. Unlike downhill and slalom races, the cross-country event is staged as a mass start with as many as a hundred racers jockeying for position at the starting gun. The bikes balance lightweight frames and components with stability and maneuverability.

FORKS AND SUSPENSIONS: Front suspensions are now almost a given on at least 90 percent of all courses. Since standard factory setups are for cross-country, few, if any, changes in equipment need to be made to most average to top-of-the-line bikes in order to race them. Dual suspensions are more common now on the race circuits, as more riders opt for comfort and performance over slightly lighter weight. Many practical recreational riders are also using the dual suspensions to improve their descending.

BRAKES: The new Shimano V-brake should be the rage for the next few years. This is undoubtedly the strongest mechanical brake on the market.

PEDALS: Cross-country riders prefer the smaller, lighter-bodied clipless design. Toe straps and clips have all but disappeared from the racing scene.

TIRES: Tires are typically dictated by the type of race and the conditions. (See page 17 under "Surface Conditions.") Generally, cross-country riders will use narrower knobbies and even less tread, like the new, ideal-condition sparse-tread tires, to improve speed.

SEAT HEIGHT: Riders are set up with higher saddle positions, which provides them with the greater leverage of the big muscles; this is especially important for the long, and sometimes brutal, climbs.

CHAPTER 12

The Psychic Rewards

*No psychic reward can ever be so powerful as winning a dare
with yourself.*
—Norman Mailer, *The Executioner's Song*

Off-road wisdom borrows next to nothing from traditional
hard-core road-bike discipline. In proper gonzo fashion, my
first trail tutor nearly a lifetime ago advised me this way:

Forget all that pain-and-gain roadie crap. Get sky, get
high, and have a kick.

The roots of mountain biking were nurtured in the fertile
soil of the hip 1970s. Hitting the trail with loosened inhibitions
set the stage for a generation of fun-loving, fearless mountain
bikers. Over the years the names and faces of riding partners
may have changed, but most of the trails, if they are still open
to us, remain the same, as does the spirit of adventure.

In this book I've emphasized fun and not white-knuckled
fear. I encourage an enthusiastic, winning attitude that confirms
"I can," "I will," "I must," instead of "I'll try" or "I think I can."
Even "trying," by its very definition, is a watered-down admis-
sion of projected failure. If our thoughts and ideas are positive,
so go our rides, so go our lives.

Most mountain bikers agree that climbing is the most difficult part of the sport. Attitude can help. I recommend several
methods for getting into the right frame of mind. The first is
"self-talk." The power of self-talk can be illustrated with the following example: Pick a friend, and ask him or her to hold out
both arms in front of the body. Now tell your friend to repeat
the following: "I hate these climbs; I've never been good at

climbing." At the same time, try pushing those arms down and make note of the resistance offered. Now try the same thing with a positive affirmation: "I'm a great climber; I can climb with anyone; I love climbing." Notice the difference? A bit more resistance perhaps? I thought so. Imagine what such positive self-talk can do for you when you are trying to hang with your buds on a killer grade—or the same condition in a race. My approach to these positive affirmations is simple: I write them down on the backs of business cards and carry them around with me in my pocket. When I need a mental boost—such as when preparing for a race or selling a sponsor—I pull them out and recite the affirmations. This procedure has become as regular as brushing my teeth.

The next method for gaining a positive attitude is more complex. My experience has been that only about 10 percent of what actually happens on the trail affects us, and that the other 90 percent involves how we react to what is happening. In other words, most of us have the potential to do amazing things on these bikes, if—and here's the biggie—we can simply bypass the fear factor.

Fear and a lack of confidence get in the way of progress. In fact, fear is the biggest cause of accidents. Most of us look at a super-tricky descent and say, "No way can I make that." When we try, we concentrate on the danger, the ugly wrong line, or any of a number of fumbling negatives. We should be focused on the correct line instead of getting hung up on the penalty of failure.

The following road story will illustrate the point. I once found myself in a breakaway with a young man who, although an excellent rider, hadn't had many appearances on the winner's podium. On this particular occasion he was riding hell-bent and the equal of any of us in a four-man break from the main bunch. Another of our breakaway partners, who knew the guy's history but realized he was still a threat, finally looked over at him—straight in the eye—with a shocked expression and yelled, "What the hell *you* doing here?"

Being next to the poor chump I could read the indecision in his face. Fear of failure, triggered by the suggestion of a repeated similar experience, was all it took to kick off his spiral of self-destruction. Sure enough, in predictable fashion his "bummer mechanism" took over and in no more than a few seconds he was struggling. His strong and confident demeanor dissolved, and he soon gave in to the ghost of self-doubt completely and was dropped off the back.

We all have our own stories of psychic defeats and victories. My introduction to mountain biking started in northern California at the 1982 Whiskeytown Downhill, a forty-plus-mile ritualistic adventure that was anything but downhill. I started the race on a dare and finished with my ego on life support. Granted, I was very tired, maybe even delirious after about a hundred endos (okay, maybe only five), but I recall realizing that even though I bombed in the race, I still won that dare with myself. After twelve years that revelation seems more important than all the world titles and accolades, whether spiritual, hormonal, or IRS refunds—none before or since has ever quite measured up to winning that first dare with myself.

Winning those personal victories feels good because it unleashes endorphins that make you high, which, incidentally, is the same reason dogs hold their heads out of car windows. Of course, any born-again type-A personality will tell you that this endorphin high is one of life's richest human experiences.

Baron Pierre de Coubertin, the founder of the modern Olympic Games, cut to the essence of this natural high in his oft-quoted statement about the value of the Olympics:

> The most important thing in the Olympics is not to win, but to take part. Just as the most important thing in life is not the triumph but the struggle. The essential thing is not to have conquered, but to have fought well.

If you are looking for that spirit today, forget the Olympics: All you will find is a media circus and a gold count. Look instead to your own spectacle of human achievement, which can easily be measured on the nearest single-track trail.

Over the years, I have come to believe that the purest expression of victory is measured in personal fortitude. Nothing impresses me more than the self-determination and will of people who get up daily and repeat difficult, sometimes thankless personal training. Some of us have discovered that occasionally mixing it up with a small dose of competitive spirit is the perfect recipe for enlightenment.

There have been times after a great training ride—usually an instructional bash with my students—when I have thought how such efforts seem, mentally and emotionally, more stimulating than races. At such times it seems as if racing, with all the associated stress and, sometimes, grief, is perhaps not the healthiest use of energy. In fact, I think racing sometimes gets in the way of training. Racing is like a jolt of pure adrenaline, a for-the-moment rush of vitality that leaves you spent, while training holds the greater purpose of longevity.

When it comes to competition, many of us still cross finish lines to beat other people, to make others lose. The real winners cross finish lines regardless of places—for themselves, in order to tell a good story and trace back all the obtuse and unlikely elements of a ride.

Achieving this sort of self-fulfilling prophecy is no different from learning to leap both wheels over obstacles. Successful completion of a technical skill involves plenty of positive reinforcement in order to boost confidence. Good dirt dogs learn to connect, not to control. When you learn to connect, you stop trying to cheat gravity. It doesn't matter if you're a beginner or an expert, successful downhill maneuvering of a mountain bike requires a healthy measure of self-confidence bordering on blind bravado. With any trail experience at all you probably discovered early on that your learning curve lurches upward when you relax and falters like a drunk on glare ice with the first tremor of self-doubt.

One of the most successful athletes I have coached was a precocious fourteen-year-old who eventually went on to win a score of junior national road and track championships. When I first introduced Denise Mueller to the trail, however, she reacted to steep sections by dismounting and tiptoeing down the slope as if on eggshells. Little by little, I got her to trust her instincts, and gradually she began to let go. Less than three years later, she won the silver medal in the World Downhill Championships in Italy. Current world champion Leigh Donovan confesses to having had the same fear of speed in the beginning.

All of us have crawled down slopes with clenched teeth, fingernailing the grips in a death clutch, muscles tight as piano wires. Needless to say, this sort of fear-driven experience is a rotten foundation for starting any new sport. This is where a technique I call "rescripting" can come in handy. To start rescripting, recall a sport of your choice—pick one you have mastered. Let's take skiing, for example.

I once saw a photo of Missy Giove descending at the Vail NORBA Nationals. All you needed to do was white-out her bike and draw in skis and poles. Her body movements would have worked equally well for either sport. Entry-level skiers are a lot like first-rung mountain bikers: They try to muscle their skis instead of relaxing with the flow. Experienced skiers know how to shift their body weight and adjust their balance to manipulate their descent. A similar connection applies to motorcycles, in-line skating, cross-country skiing, surfing, snowboarding, and, of course, mountain biking. The magic of rescripting comes from connecting the subtle body movements and motor skills from a previously mastered activity with those of a less familiar sport—in this case, riding a mountain bike. (Another hint: Quick learners have two things in common—a strong spirit of adventure and the ability to laugh at themselves. Keep your sense of humor, even as you lick your wounds.)

Getting into the right frame of mind before heading downhill can be a real challenge. It's so easy to blast off in a wash of adrenaline-sparked enthusiasm. Most of us have starting guns in our brains. Next time, try meditating first. Create a mental image of fat-tired tranquillity, some rolling fields rather than a craggy downhill slide. Focus—really focus!—on this image, then paint yourself into that scene. Colors are great stimulators of power. Try playing with a favorite color—let's call it blue-sky blue. Let the blue sky undulate slowly with your growing resolve. Now connect it with the blood in your veins and watch it begin to turn red. Feel it gathering momentum, falling, roaring toward your heart, glowing the color of molten steel. Colors are very effective when you are dealing with the introspective realm of personal pain—for example, nearing the end of a long, hard race when you are looking for images to spark that last bit of fortitude.

Now, when you mount your plastic, aluminum, or steel steed, think about flowing down the trail in full suspension. For the nonmeditator. No problem. I'll risk public stoning by suggesting you pop a cold one—just one, now—before the ride. I know plenty of dirt artists who swear that such mild sedation is the best way to loosen inhibitions, a key factor in personal experimentation.

Try to relax, and don't try to control anything—nobody's ever completely in charge. Even if you get it right this time, sooner or later you're going to go down. Why not let go and turn these wipeouts into learning opportunities? Don't dwell on the fear of failure. Instead, surround yourself with positive, but not pushy, people. When success comes—and it will come—slap on a high five, smile big, and pretend you have arrived. Having done it once, you will do it again, and again, each time improving and reinforcing the technical skill at hand. With each mastery of a particular maneuver, remember that the path to fun is paved, if not littered, with an ever-widening assortment of obstacles.

The purpose of this book has been is to ground you in the basics, but beware: There is something dangerously primal about this dirty sport. Before you know it, you may find yourself forging back into your childhood, returning home covered with mud, and feeling slightly giddier than big people are supposed to feel.

APPENDIX A

Stretching

STAYING LOOSE: A USER-FRIENDLY GUIDE TO TURNING FLEXIBILITY INTO SPEED

Stretching is a lot like religion. Some of us are fervent believers, while some of us give it lip service with a few measly toe touches or hamstring stretches. Others don't believe in it at all. Come on, people: We all need to stretch.

The reasons for incorporating stretching into our daily lives go way beyond just being good mountain-bike riders. Stretching keeps the body youthful, reduces the chance of injury, and vastly speeds recovery from workouts. Plus, flexible muscles perform better.

For those of us who beat up our bodies in the dirt, reducing the chance of (or speeding the recovery from) an injury is the most compelling reason for making stretching as routine as pumping up our tires. Cycling coaches may have different views on performance training, but few would advise training through an injury. Many cycling-related injuries are caused by nothing more than muscles that finally get so tight they rub on bones and tissues, thus causing inflammation.

If the above situation sounds vaguely familiar, you may be asking yourself why these injuries always seem to come back or, worse yet, become chronic. The answer is because the underlying problem is not being addressed. Balancing muscle strength with overall flexibility is the greatest insurance policy against overuse injuries.

If you follow this program, you will be able to tolerate more lactic acid and cover more miles faster. The other side of this coin has to do with injury recovery. If you have knee pain caused by an inflexible iliotibial band, stretching that tendon will speed the recovery. Continuing to stretch the surrounding musculature will prevent the condition from coming back.

Just in case the first two reasons were not enough to get your attention. Here's another: Being more flexible will improve your performance by increasing your strength, endurance, and psychological ability. The mountain biker with the more flexible muscles has the advantage. Lactic acid has a destructive effect on skeletal muscle myofibrils, which are the smallest functioning muscle units. Lactic acid impedes coordination and diminishes the ability of the body's contractile protein to contract. In other words, the contractile protein is denatured by high levels of lactic acid in the blood, so you go slower. With the addition of flexibility training, the individual myofibrils are stretched significantly. Dirt dogs who take the time to stretch will have longer, more flexible myofibrils, which, when exposed to lactic acid, will not shorten as much as short myofibrils that have not undergone flexibility training. A well-stretched cyclist will be able to generate more force at the end of a given event than a rider who thinks stretching is for sissies.

Finally, flexibility training allows you to develop kinesthetic sense—that is, the ability to know what your body is doing at any given time. Pedal-stroke refinement, according to our School of Champions stretching coach, Dr. Morris Mann, is "next to impossible without a strong sense of kinesthetics." While flexibility training does not teach you to master smooth pedaling, it does help you know where your body is at any given time, thus improving coordination and control.

Most cyclists know that flexibility is important, but though many claim to stretch, what they really mean is that while they are procrastinating about getting on the bike they lean against a tree for a few seconds, then pull their foot behind them once or twice. Instead, what you need is a systematic way to stretch all the muscles required for pedaling.

Before you begin your stretching debut, let's take a look at the three main types of stretching. For years ballistic stretching was assumed to be the way to go. Ballistic stretching is when you bounce and hurl yourself into the stretch. There is a high chance of injury, and the stretch is actually thwarted by the muscle's reflex to tighten in response to fast movement. The body is tightening to protect itself. In the 1970s and '80s people saw the value in performing slower stretches and holding those stretches. Books like *Stretching*, by Bob Anderson, became million-copy sellers. This is still the most popular method of stretching, but now in the '90s a different form of stretching is getting impressive results. This method is called active isolated stretching, or AI. The best description of AI stretching is that it seems to combine all the best aspects of yoga, ballistic, and static stretching without any drawbacks. Active isolation stretching was developed twenty-five years ago by Aaron Mattes, who was looking for a specific method of lengthening muscles and connective tissue, or fascia. His book, published in 1995, is entitled *Active Isolated Stretching*. Thousands of athletes in all sports have improved performance and decreased tissue soreness and injury employing AI stretching techniques.

The principle of active isolated stretching is rooted in basic physiology. Use one muscle to start moving the limb, and the opposing muscle relaxes. Think about it: When you contract the biceps, the triceps must relax to allow your arm to move. In AI, each stretch is taken as far as the opposing muscle can move, and then assistance takes it farther. You hold the stretch for 2 seconds and repeat it for 8 to 10 contractions. The reason for holding for 2 seconds is to get beyond the muscle's initial reflexive tightening in response to the stretch. Each successive repeat usually allows for increased range of motion.

My goal for this chapter is to arouse your curiosity and get you to try some active isolation stretches. The stretches shown here are those we practice and teach at the School of Champions. Personal instruction is a valuable part of an effective stretching program. Some health clubs offer good classes on stretching, and most qualified trainers can help you improve your flexibility, which is really the core of your athleticism, a vital key to kick-ass mountain biking. If you choose to go it alone, here are eleven stretches that you'll learn to love.

Note: With the exception of the back bend, hold each stretch for 2 seconds and do 8 to 10 repeats. It may feel awkward at first, but stretching is worth the time and effort. If you are caught in a time squeeze, it will be well worth cutting back your ride by 20 minutes to fit in stretching.

1. **Hamstring warm-up stretch.** Lie on your back and pull your knees to your armpits. Hold for 2 seconds and repeat 8 to 10 times.

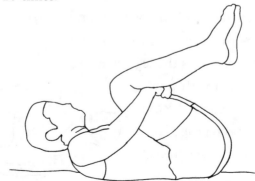

2. **Hamstring stretch.** Lie on your back and engage your quad muscles to lift one leg up. Use your hands, a belt, a rope, or an inner tube to assist at the end of the movement. Hold for 2 seconds and repeat 8 to 10 times for each leg.

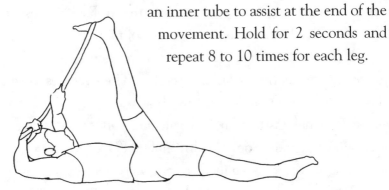

3. **Gluteus and buttock stretch.** Lie on your back, pull your knee to your chest with your hands, a belt, a rope, or an inner tube, and sweep your foot across your body. Hold for 2 seconds and repeat 8 to 10 times for each leg.

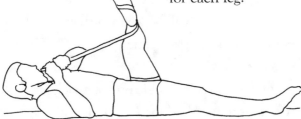

4. **Quad stretch.** Lie on one side and engage the hamstring to move the top leg back. As the leg comes back, assist with your hand. Hold for 2 seconds and repeat 8 to 10 times for each leg.

5. **Hip abductor and iliotibial band stretch.** Lying on your back, contract your hip adductors (inner thigh) to pull one leg to the opposite side. Hold for 2 seconds and repeat 8 to 10 times for each leg.

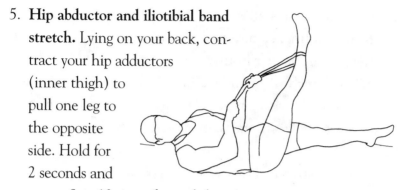

6. **Hip adductor and groin stretch.** Lying on your back, contract the hip abductors (outer thigh) to pull one leg out to the side, keeping the leg close to the ground. Hold for 2 seconds and repeat 8 to 10 times for each leg.

7. **External hip rotators** are critical for accessing the deep hip muscles so important in turning over big gears. Lying on your back, bring one knee up and pull to the inside, thus rotating the hip to the outside. Hold for 2 seconds and repeat 8 to 10 times for each leg. Vary the position to work the full range of motion.

8. The calf requires a series of three exercises to stretch the soleus, gastrocnemius, and Achilles tendon. All three stretches are similar in that you engage the anterior tibialis muscle, which is the muscle in the front of the shin, then assist with hands or rope to facilitate the stretch. Repeat each stretch 8 to 10 times, then switch legs.

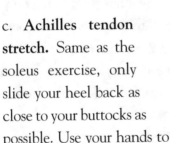

a. **Soleus stretch.** From a seated position with your legs out in front of you, slide one heel back to the knee of the opposing leg (about halfway back). Engage the anterior tibialis of the bent leg and assist with your hands to feel the stretch.

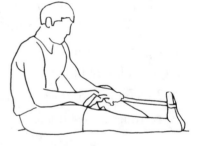

b. **Gastrocnemius stretch.** While you are in the same position as the previous exercise, stretch the muscles in the leg that is flat on the ground. Use your hands or a rope to assist with the stretch.

c. **Achilles tendon stretch.** Same as the soleus exercise, only slide your heel back as close to your buttocks as possible. Use your hands to assist with the stretch after engaging the anterior tibialis.

9. **Neck stretch.** One of the biggest complaints we hear from cyclists is about pain in the upper neck region; this stretch will greatly reduce these symptoms. Sitting or standing with your head aligned straight ahead, pull the head to the left with two fingers. Hold for 2 seconds. Repeat to the right, and perform 8 to 10 reps on each side. Finally, proceed with the same routine to the front.

10. **Back bend.** This helps counteract the effects of leaning into a bike for hours of trail riding on rough terrain.

11. **Standing side stretch.** With hands behind your head, contract the muscles on one side and stretch the opposite side. Hold each side stretch for 2 seconds. Repeat 8 to 10 times on each side.

Weight Training

CONDITIONING/STRENGTH/POWER/ MAINTENANCE

The most complete method of lifting your performance level in mountain biking is to start lifting weights. Break your program up into four separate phases. Each phase has specific objectives and lasts 6 to 8 weeks. The first, the conditioning phase, tones the cycling muscles with high repetitions and light weights. Ideally, this phase should start in October, after the regular riding or racing season has drawn to a close. The second, the strength phase, works the muscles to overload with maximum lifting capacity, increasing the weight and decreasing the number of reps. The third, the power phase, progressively expands your strength and muscular endurance with more actual biking. The fourth and final phase is maintenance. The goal of the maintenance phase is to return to the gym once a week to hold muscle tone and stabilize your hard-earned strength and power.

Begin each workout by stretching. Lifting weights without stretching shortens your muscles and makes them less effective. As you begin lifting, work the large muscle groups first. This pumps more blood into the rest of the body. In the strength phase, remember to always work the muscle group to overload. The last few reps are the most critical for developing strength. While maximum results come from working the upper and lower body on alternate days, most of us usually do a full-body workout to have more time on the bike.

When referring to the endurance element of weight train-ing we sometimes use "strength" and "power" interchangeably, yet they have different meanings. "Strength-based endurance" refers to the amount of time you can continue exercising a given muscle group. "Power-based endurance" is the ability to use strength in a fast or explosive manner for a short duration. Improved strength means better coordination of intramuscular forces, thus producing a stronger pull. Better coordination means recruiting more muscle fibers and more efficient pedaling. To develop strength, you need to lift heavy weights slowly. This develops slow-twitch, or endurance, muscle fibers. Power and speed, conversely, are produced by lifting the same weight faster. This charges the fast-twitch, or speed, muscle fibers. Another important feature of both the strength and power phases is an "active memory" supplement in which you ride your bike to and from the gym, or before and after each weight workout. It is especially important to warm up the muscles with extra blood flow, then crank up the rpms after the workout to remind them of their true purpose.

Since both lifting free weights and using machines load the muscles in a linear plane, supplementary cycling will reinforce the more complicated motor response of pedaling. The biking will build a higher tolerance to lactic acid in your blood and hasten recovery.

The type of apparatus used for your weight training is a personal choice. Each device has advantages and disadvantages. Machine weights are the easiest to use and can be supplemented with free weights. When getting to a gym is a problem, my favorite training tool is the Bobby Hinds Lifeline Gym. The Lifeline is a simple, inexpensive, portable gym consisting of a collapsible bar and rubber stretch cords. If you get creative and actually read the instruction booklet or plug in the video, you can use the Lifeline to work quite a few muscle groups. The best thing about the Lifeline is you can pitch it into your suitcase and use it anywhere, anytime. You can order a Lifeline by calling (800) 553-6633.

Conditioning Phase. Following the suggestions
below, condition yourself with 6 to 8 weeks of strength training, gradually increasing the weight by 10 to 15 percent. As with each phase, concentrate on form and breathing. Avoid jerking the weight, perform each rep in a slow and systematic fashion, and work to overload. Exhale completely on the flexion cycle and recover in a smooth, rhythmic fashion on the extension.

Period:	6 to 8 weeks
Days per week:	2
Intensity:	Weight gradually increases by 10 to 15 percent.
Repetitions:	Weeks 1–3: 10 to 12; Weeks 4–8: 15 to 20
Sets:	2 or 3
Ideal cycling:	Easy, fun rides, 3 to 4 days per week; road and off-road; no agenda; mix it up with some jogging.

MUSCLES

Stomach and obliques:	Crunches, bicycle crunches—pumping the legs as if on a bicycle while doing crunches, and with hips adjusted at an angle to work obliques.
Lower back:	Hyperextensions.
Quadriceps:	Leg extensions—one leg at a time (or single-leg) to ensure equal strength in both legs. Free-weight squats—work with a trainer to ensure proper form.
Hamstrings:	Leg curls—single-leg.
Glutes:	Walking lunges, hack squats, leg-press machine.

Calves:	Toe raises.
Adductors:	Side leg pulls.
Abductors:	Side leg pushes.
Hip flexors (psoas, iliacus, and tensor fascia):	Sprinter's high-knee lunges with pulley machine or the Lifeline gym.
Biceps:	Biceps curls.
Triceps:	Triceps curls.
Shoulders:	Upright rows.
Chest:	Bench presses.
Upper back:	Lat pulldowns.

Strength Phase. During the strength phase, increase your weights by another 10 to 15 percent, but be careful to avoid straining the muscles excessively.

Period:	6 to 8 weeks
Days per week:	2 or 3
Intensity:	Weight gradually increases by 10 to 15 percent.
Repetitions:	10 to 12
Sets:	2 or 3
Ideal cycling:	Longer rides, road and off-road. Increase ride volume and intensity by 25 percent. (See appendix E on zone training.)

MUSCLES

Stomach and obliques:	Bicycle crunches and lying leg raises.
Lower back:	Hyperextensions.
Quadriceps:	Leg extensions (single, then double), squats.

Hamstrings:	Leg curls (single, then double).
Glutes:	Lunges, hack squats, leg-press machine.
Calves:	Toe raises—go full range up and down.
Adductors:	Side leg pulls.
Abductors:	Side leg pushes.
Hip flexors:	Forward lunges using pulley machine or Lifeline Gym.
Biceps:	Biceps curls.
Triceps:	Triceps curls.
Shoulders:	Upright rows.
Chest:	Bench presses.
Upper back:	Lat pulldowns.

Power Phase. Emphasize a quick advancing movement on the lifting portion of the exercise, then a slow return to the base. Perform all exercises to overload. Remember to concentrate on rhythmic breathing. End each workout with a few high-rpm bike miles to reinforce muscle memory.

Period:	6 to 8 weeks
Days per week:	2 or 3
Intensity:	Weight gradually increases 5 to 10 percent by week 4 but stabilizes after that time.
Repetitions:	10 to 12
Sets:	Lower body—3 or 4 Upper body—1 or 2
Ideal cycling:	One long ride per week; include more technical off-road routes and increase training volume and intensity. Twice per week include 8 to 10 2-minute high-intensity intervals or ride full race pace with a group.

Cycling during program:	Warm up slowly for 5 minutes, then gradually pick up the tempo to get the blood flowing.

MUSCLES

Stomach and obliques:	Sit-ups, crunches, bike crunches, reverse and side crunches.
Lower back:	Hyperextensions.
Glutes:	Hack squats, leg-press machine, deep walking lunges (across a room) with handheld weights. Keep torso straight.
Hip Flexors:	One-leg pedaling; target isolation with pulley machine.
Quadriceps:	Lunges and hack squats.
Upper (rectus femoris) and Mid (vastus lateralis):	Leg-press machine.
Lower (vastus medialis):	Leg extensions with toes pointed in.
All:	Deep squats with good form.
Hamstrings:	Leg curls—single- and double-leg.
Calves (gastrocnemius and soleus):	Toe raises—full range of motion, deep and high.
Adductors:	Side leg pulls, machine or Lifeline.
Abductors:	Side leg pushes, machine or Lifeline.
Biceps:	Curls, free-weight or machine.
Triceps:	Free-weight or machine.
Shoulders:	Machine, free weights, Lifeline.
Chest:	Machine or free-weight bench presses.
Upper back:	Lat pulldowns.

Maintenance Phase. This is the final segment of the program. You will begin gradually *decreasing* the volume of weight by 15 to 20 percent. Work out 1 or 2 days per week for the duration of the year. This phase of your training should be viewed as an opportunity to strengthen your resolve. Treat these workouts as relaxed confidence builders. Not only are you strengthening the cycling muscles, you are building determination, which is one of those elusive keys to success.

Period:	12 to 16 weeks
Days per week:	1 or 2
Intensity:	Weight gradually decreases by 15 to 20 percent.
Repetitions:	First workout—10 to 12, second—15 to 20. Reduce weight by 5 to 10 percent on second workout.
Sets:	Lower body—3 or 4 Upper body—1
Ideal cycling:	Shorter, faster intervals; fartlek; hill repeats on and off-road.
Muscles:	(See "Strength phase" above.)

Nutrition

I get all the exercise I need lifting the caskets of my exercising friends.

—Mark Twain

SUPPLEMENTING TO SURVIVE

Is there anyone among us who has not absorbed a dose of medical dogma about the goodness of cycling as a form of exercise? So, what's the problem? In a nutshell, some of us may be rolling time bombs. Statistics indicate that thousands of athletes—of all ages—drop dead each year, some from no apparent reason, others from various forms of cancer, heart disease, or neurological disorders.

The suspect? A shortage of full-spectrum nutritional elements, something that supplementation can provide. Full-spectrum nutrition is broadly defined as an abundant supply of seventy-two minerals, sixteen vitamins, and eight to twelve amino acids. Even though the role of nutrition in athletic performance is endlessly documented, a small but determined group of health-care professionals is convinced that thus far we are only being given part of the story. Most public information revolves around just a smattering of "high-profile" nutrients, while ignoring the fact that we need about a hundred others every day. There is plenty of evidence to support full-spectrum nutrition as the best way to enhance your athletic performance. Far more important to all of us than athletic performance, however, should be longevity.

IT HAPPENS TO US

In 1981 the cycling community mourned the untimely death of national team rider Bob Cook. Bob was in his twenties. More recently, Fred Lebow, fifty-six, an avid runner and the founder of the New York Marathon, and Wilma Rudolph, fifty-four, a triple gold medal track star, also expired. What all three had in common was brain cancer, a condition that can be produced in lab animals by placing them on a diet deficient in the trace mineral gallium. America's best miler, national record holder Steve Scott, believes his shotgun approach to nutrition was a factor when he came down with testicular cancer, which, incidentally, is the same horror that has sidelined U.S. road star Lance Armstrong. For many athletes, it is inevitable that a biochemical imbalance will occur when high volumes of one nutrient are taken in the absence of others. Steve was lucky; the problem was discovered in the early stages, and his recovery regimen of full-spectrum nutrition got him back on track. Steve was a candidate for the 1996 Olympic team and barely missed qualifying at age forty.

Yet other athletes have not been so fortunate. Collegiate hoop star Hank Gathers from Loyola Marymount, in Los Angeles, collapsed and died of cardiomyopathy on the court during the "March Madness" play-offs in 1990. He was twenty-three. It seems logical that a lesson could be learned from this young man's tragic death, but in April 1993 Reggie Lewis, the twenty-seven-year-old captain of the Boston Celtics, collapsed on the court, also diagnosed with cardiomyopathy. Even his

"Dream Team" of cardiologists couldn't save the sixty-five-million-dollar star: Just three months later he again collapsed on the court, and this time he died. The list goes on, in horrible obedience to the laws of biochemistry. Thirty-one-year-old boxing champion Evander Holyfield was forced to end his career by the same problem. Holyfield proved to be the enlightened one. With a new program complete with essential vitamins and minerals, including the trace mineral selenium, he has successfully returned to the ring.

What is interesting to note is that back in 1950s veterinary scientists conducting animal studies found that the absence of the trace mineral selenium could lead to a variety of diseases, including cardiomyopathy. This saved a lot of farm animals, but, sadly, the information was largely ignored by the medical community.

The media and the food industry can share the blame for the intense publicity given to vitamins in lieu of other nutrients, namely minerals. With the exception of major structural and electrolyte minerals, such as calcium, magnesium, potassium, sodium, iron, and chloride, very little information has been publicized regarding this group of nutrients that make up two-thirds of all essential substances in our bodies. Many nutritionists believe that establishing basic requirements for vitamins and minerals is just the start. Once we meet the basic needs, the rest of the nutritional puzzle is still incomplete.

CELLULAR DAMAGE

In coaching mountain bikers to peak performance, I encourage my athletes to supplement their diets with seventy-two minerals, sixteen vitamins, twelve essential amino acids, and three fatty acids—nutrients responsible for countless biological activities within the body.

A strong premise of this principle is that active cyclists have nutritional requirements greater than those of most couch potatoes. Sustained activity and the subsequent breakdown and repair of tissue is comparable with wearing out and replacing bike parts. Think about what happens to the drivetrain of your bike, for example, when an old chain begins to stretch and doesn't get replaced. In the body, this breakdown of tissues, along with the increased production of biochemicals such as hormones, is called catabolism. The search for the optimum safe anticatabolic starts with a host of nutrients, many of them minerals. Daily replacement of these nutrients, which are literally sweated out of the body, plays a big part in both performance and subsequent recovery. So-called sports drinks claim to provide the nutrients lost during exercise while replacing fluids, yet a closer examination of many of these drinks shows that they contain little more than water, sugar, and two or three electrolytes. A good diet and adequate rest are critical, but complete mineralization of the body is the catalyst that gives performance lasting substance.

FREE RADICALS

Free radicals are not left-wingers left over from the 1960s, although their disruption of cellular functions can create an infinitely more personal form of anarchy. Free radicals are roving molecules that contain unstable electrons. These free radicals come from either pollutants or our own bodies functions; and left unchecked, they can result in a host of physical short circuits, the worst-case scenario being cancer. Although the smoking gun is still absent, growing research suggests that free radicals are a key player in Parkinson's disease and other neurological disorders commonly associated with aging. Motor disturbances have for some time been known to stem from the destruction of certain nerve cells in the brain. That's why anti-oxidants are so vital to cell function; they are the scavengers that get rid of the free radicals for us.

CAN'T I JUST EAT A BALANCED DIET?

Of all the myths perpetually foisted on us, none is more baseless than the food industry's fib about getting all of our nutrients from balanced diets. First, only about 9 percent of the population eats a balanced diet. Second, it is a well-grounded fact that our foods do not contain anywhere close to the hundred-odd essential nutrients. The reason is simple: The soils where the foods are grown are largely depleted of these elements. Deficiencies in these micro trace minerals do not always produce immediate noticeable symptoms. However, their prolonged absence, combined with the physical and emotional stress of athletic performance, can lead to metabolic breakdowns with potentially health-compromising side effects.

While science has yet to isolate and identify the biochemical roles of all the minerals in our internal chemistry, experience has taught us that nature doesn't play dice with us, and nothing happens without a reason. The importance of vitamins was discovered not so very long ago. The B-complex group of vitamins was isolated and identified long before the biological functions of many of them were determined.

Synergy, or the intrinsic relationship between substances, has long been established for vitamins and amino acids; we are now finding the same holds true for minerals. There is a common false belief that just because micro trace elements are needed in extremely small amounts, this somehow negates their importance. In fact, the quality of nutrients is far more important than the quantity. Recent scientific studies show conclusively that if even one of the essential minerals is deficient, the others cannot do their jobs.

AVOIDING THE EXPENSIVE-URINE SYNDROME

In truth, if we were to get all of the essential ingredients to promote vitality and longevity, we would literally need to carry around a steamer trunk full of vitamins and minerals. The cost of these supplements would run three to five hundred dollars per month. Additionally, we would need some advanced product knowledge in order to get the correct dosage. A third problem concerns absorbability. Supplements are by no means created equal. The degree of absorbability depends on their structure. Minerals come in one of three forms: metallic, chelated, or colloidal. Metallic minerals are extremely poorly absorbed and give good meaning to the term "expensive urine." Chelated vitamins and minerals are reduced in form and bound to an amino acid and are more absorbable; but by far the most usable form of a mineral is the liquid colloidal. Inexpensive, organic colloidal elements are processed from living plants. They are converted to a negative electrical charge, making them almost completely absorbable at the cellular level.

History has much to teach us about supplementation. The peoples of every continent from antiquity forward have relied on the healing powers of minerals and herbs. My favorite examples of civilizations that exist today with a high degree of health and longevity include the Eastern European Georgians, the Hunzukuts of Hunza, and the Titicacans of Peru, all of whom have an average life span two or three decades longer than any "civilized" people. The single link between all of these cultures can be found in their water source. In every case, the water originates in the mountains and flows through deep mineral-rich deposits laced with colloidal trace minerals from plant matter compressed for millions of years. Give colloidal minerals a try; the odds are you'll be quite surprised at how strong and vibrant they'll make you feel.

Since we know that what holds true for the "average" sedentary person is multiplied many times in the body of a training cyclist, the synergy of nutrient relationships becomes even more vital. Meet a few of the major minerals and a few of their supporting cast of trace minerals. There are seventy-two in total, and if sweat is part of your lifestyle, they need to be replaced daily.

Calcium: A 150-pound athlete contains around 3 pounds of calcium, 99 percent of which is found in the bones. The remaining 1 percent performs hundreds of biochemical chores, including controlling nerve impulses from the brain to muscles. Calcium is a good example of nutritional synergy at work. To adequately utilize calcium, the body needs magnesium, silicon, fluoride, zinc, copper, boron, manganese, phosphorus, and vitamin D.

Potassium is rapidly excreted through sweat, putting athletes at greater risk than the rest of the population. Potassium deficits have devastated the performance of many endurance athletes, yet try finding any significant amount of it in most "sports drinks."

Zinc is necessary for the production of many essential enzymes that power digestion, cell growth, and the production of testosterone. A deficiency of zinc for as little as a week retards muscle growth and weakens the immune system.

Copper is another very important mineral for the athlete since it, too, is responsible for the production of numerous enzymes, including those that produce noradrenaline, the most important energy hormone. Blood tests of athletes show that many are copper deficient, partly because reserves are rapidly depleted during high-intensity training. Copper is also a factor in the absorption of many minerals, including calcium.

Manganese is necessary for the formation of bone and cartilage. It is also involved in glucose metabolism, a very important mechanism in the body of an athlete.

Chromium is responsible for insulin production, fatty acid metabolism, and muscle growth. Chromium assists in glucose metabolism and the conversion of stored energy into usable muscle fuel. It is also responsible for metabolism because of its activity in the Krebs energy cycle.

Iodine is necessary for making thyroid hormones. These hormones control all the energy in the body, making iodine tops on the list of athletic requirements. Small deficiencies of iodine can lead to loss of performance because of low production of energy. Large deficiencies can cause thyroid problems.

Boron is essential for the uptake and conversion of calcium. Boron also assists in the manufacture of natural steroidal hormones. Rather than take the synthetic counterparts with a host of side effects, would it not be better to encourage the body's production of its own natural steroids? These hydroxyl groups, are the precursors to hormones that govern calcium and magnesium metabolism in the bones as well as muscle growth.

Recommended reading:
Self Health: The Complete Guide to Optimal Wellness, by Dr. Steven Whiting (available from the School of Champions).

APPENDIX D

BreathPlay

LESSONS FROM AN EDGE PLAYER

"Who the hell is this guy Ian Jackson?" That was the way one of my fellow Ironman competitors expressed his intimidation before the start of the 1981 event. Jackson had announced his confidence of a win in the press, and given the infantile level of the sport back then, nearly everyone could be considered a threat. Because we were worlds apart, I was especially intrigued with his creative approach to cycling. I was submerged in physical prowess, while he dealt in the metaphysical and sublime. At first, when I won the event and Ian finished well back in the field, I thought I had the edge, but later I came to realize I had only scratched the surface of the broader field of human performance.

I got my chance to work with Jackson during a seminar we were conducting at a boys' prep school in Tennessee. The subject of this program was the concept of turning sports sense into life sense. While I mind-boggled the kids with my forty-hour-a-week preparation to set the twenty-four-hour cycling endurance record, Jackson dealt with an idea he called "BreathPlay" and how the body-mind connection had fueled his race. Never mind the fact that he didn't even race; the students empathized with him and let loose a barrage of questions about the mental part of training and racing. This was a perfect lead-in for Jackson to connect the breathing with his favorite subject—hypnosis, and its power to eliminate unconscious performance blocks. He spoke highly of his teacher Milton Erickson, whom he believed was the world's foremost hypnotherapist. He concluded our session by hypnotizing the entire audience.

We had the afternoon off, and I was intent on pumping Jackson about this hypnosis thing. He seemed intent, though, on diverting my interest to BreathPlay. "Experience teaches better than talk," he said. I was resistant. Only because I felt obligated did I agree to let him coach me in basic BreathPlay on a bike ride. The fact was that I had developed a successful approach to cycling and had no desire to fix what already worked. I listened halfheartedly to his explanation.

He started with what he called "UpsideDown" breathing and had me explore switching from the usual pattern of sucking air in and letting it out to the UpsideDown pattern of pushing air out and letting it in. It felt unnatural. Like most people, I was so used to sucking my air that it was difficult to let the in-breath just happen without working at it. Jackson was a good teacher; he had his skill so finely tuned that it was easy to see where the exercise was taking us. He made his breathing clearly audible so that I could catch what he was doing. He made a smooth hissing or whooshing sound as he breathed out and an easy *aaah* as he breathed in. He had me watching closely from the side of the road as he pulled his belly way back with that hissing out-breath and then let it round out with that aaahing in-breath. The real clincher was the way he rode away from me on the hills with each extension of out-breath. Once I was reasonably familiar with UpsideDown breathing, he led me through some explorations of the SwitchSide breathing, comparing the technique to shifting gears on the bike. The sounds of the rhythms of the breathing, he explained, were like gears that would help accelerate the early learning.

We started with a 3/2 (out/in) rhythm, counting each pedal stroke like a footstep and putting steps in the breathing sounds to make a clear connection between the breathing and the pedaling. We fit each out-breath into three pedal strokes by putting three steps or stages into the out-breath sound: "hisss-ssss-ssss." We fit each in-breath into two pedal strokes by putting two steps into the sound: "aaaa-aaah."

I remember thinking there was something hypnotic about that recurring rhythm of sound: hsss-ssss-ssss, aaaa-aaah; hsss-ssss-ssss, aaaa-aaah. It was a big help to have him right there with me, sounding out the pattern in perfect synchrony with each pedal stroke. I was able to get into the rhythm and feel the surge of extra power working right away.

After I'd tried the 3/2 (out/in) rhythm for a while, he had me try a few other rhythms, like 2/1 (out/in) for climbing hills and 4/3 (out/in) for a downwind section. This was powerful stuff, but still I found myself resisting. I fully intended to get back into the tried-and-true unconscious breathing that had worked just fine for me in the past. I was looking forward to my next solo ride, when I was going to throw off this burdensome breathing baggage and simply work out.

But when that next solo ride came, I found that Jackson's coaching had reached deeper into my subconscious than I had realized. I set off on a familiar circuit, looking forward to four hours of easy riding, BreathPlay-free. Instead, I found myself thinking about BreathPlay in spite of myself. Within a few miles I was searching, as Jackson had suggested, for a rhythm that fit my work rate. When the variations in the workload were lower, I discovered I could stay in that same rhythm and simply change the intensity of my breathing. When the variations were more dramatic, as in hard climbing, I would shift down to a shorter rhythm, like 3/2 (out/in) or 2/1 (out/in). As the miles ticked away, the patterns became more complex. I found the odd-count breath cycles (with an odd number of pedal strokes for each complete out/in cycle) would automatically balance the work of the right and left legs. As I followed the rhythms in the pedal strokes, I got a certain satisfaction in noticing that each breath cycle ended on the opposite pedal from the one before.

Jackson had predicted that as I got more deeply into the rhythms I would find that they would tend to wash away the pain of hard work. That turned out to be true: Not only were the hills easier than I remembered, I even found myself sailing over the top using the big ring, where before I had struggled with the small one. A glance at my watch indicated that I had covered the usual four-hour course in three hours and forty-five minutes. Looking back at our first session in Tennessee, I now realize that BreathPlay was really the medium for introducing me to the deeper process of self-hypnosis.

Two years later, after a particularly harrowing experience in Baja, Mexico, in which I narrowly escaped serious injury while attempting to break the bicycle speed record, I again sought Jackson's council. I had read Milton Erickson's book *My Voice Will Go with You,* and I understood the BreathPlay system, but nothing could dispel the terror I was experiencing as a result of the near miss in Baja. A lot of money had been spent, sponsors were waiting, the project needed a conclusion, and I was feeling the pressure. Using Jackson's hypnotic BreathPlay techniques in tandem with my own creative visualization, I began to make progress. Essentially, I eliminated fear at the unconscious level. The immediate result, I am proud to say, was a Guinness world record of 152 mph in July 1985, on the Utah Salt Flats.

I have applied those mind and body techniques to enhance my performance in every athletic contest I have participated in since that day on the Salt Flats. In Jackson's book *The BreathPlay Approach to Wholelife Fitness,* another of his students, Alexi Grewal, a 1984 Olympic gold medalist, states, "This breathing [method] is the most powerful tool that can be imagined." Researcher Daniel Wojta found that when he tested groups of both BreathPlay-trained and nontrained students, the trained group realized an average increase of 7.2 percent in their VO_2 max scores and delayed their anaerobic threshold by two minutes. Wojta's simple conclusion: Breath-Play increases endurance.

As a successful elite master cyclist I harbor no illusions about my athletic ability. In terms of speed and strength, I have given up some ground, but the real excitement comes in the gain column. From a knowledgeable teacher, I have learned that the lessons of ultimate performance are as basic as breath itself.

Recommended reading:
The BreathPlay Approach to Wholelife Fitness, by Ian Jackson (available from the School of Champions).

Zone
Training

TRAINING WITH A PURPOSE

The only sure way of getting great VO_2 max* and AT[†] capabilities is to have chosen your parents wisely. Heredity aside, I
have seen measurable improvement in oxygen-carrying capacity with regular high-level training, but the onus is on you to do
the training. Here is a simple method of defining and keeping
track of your training zones.

The old standard for testing human aerobic values is the
VO_2 max test. But how many of us can recite our current
ML/KG[††] VO_2 max test score, anaerobic threshold results,
maximum heart rate, and know what the hell it all means?
While these numbers may be useful in computing lab results,
for most of us they are still just numbers. Most serious cyclists
recognize the need to train with a heart-rate monitor. The
problem is that we have no truly usable standards for measuring our training workloads.

Since heart rate, work rate, and consumption of oxygen are
all closely related, it is difficult to use pure heart rate to define
exercise levels in all phases of training. Also compounding
this problem is the factor of atmospheric conditions, which
play a part in determining overall range. Maximum heart rate
is the standard exercise physiologists usually use to derive
work intensity. In the real world of mountain-bike riding, and

---

*"VO_2 max" refers to the maximum rate of oxygen utilization during heavy exer-
cise. Your VO_2 max increases as the oxygen-delivery system is improved and the
ability of the active muscles to utilize the available oxygen is also improved.
[†]"AT" (anaerobic threshold) is the point where you reach your highest level of efficiency. At this point, regardless of workload, you can't consume any more oxygen.
[††]ML/KG VO_2 max calculations are based on the volume of oxygen in milliliters
(ML) per kilogram (KG) of body weight.

especially racing, you may see a lot of your high-end zones. Using the max heart rate as a guide, I am going to provide a more accurate description of maximum effort. For the sake of clarity I'll just refer to maximum effort as threshold heart rate, or THR. THR is especially suited for defining max efforts of about 1 hour. THR will vary depending on fitness level, but it is a fairly accurate measure of anaerobic threshold, and easily measurable with your monitor.

KEEP IT SIMPLE

When I was training to break the world land-speed record, my sponsors Gary Hooker and his partner Dave Spangler (both were world-class master endurance athletes) of Hooker Industries designed a system of defining work level that they called "heart-rate paces." By varying these paces we saw significant gains in both VO_2 max and AT, which describes the portion of VO_2 max that can be maintained aerobically.

AT training is a good method of measuring your ability to exercise at high intensity for longer durations. Working at or above the AT zone is the body's equivalent of accelerating a race car over the engine's "red line," thus losing peak power and maybe blowing the engine. The human body works in a similar manner; oxygen delivery to the muscles drops behind demand, and lactic acid invades our bodies like a swarm of hungry locusts.

QUANTIFYING THE EFFORT

Gary and Dave devised a submaximal test that I have since adapted to determine base-level fitness. The test is similar to the United States Cycling Federation protocol involving the CompuTrainer computer training system. The test is very simple and measures time, heart rate, watts, perceived breathing level on a scale of 1 to 10, speed, and gear ratio. Every half mile we bump the resistance grade by 1 percent. Our objective is to take the individual as close to maximum heart rate as possible. When the rpms drop off by more than 10 percent we stop the test. Using a calculation of .9 multiplied by the final heart rate gives us the AT. We also use .8 to determine the low side of the working AT zone. This will serve as an ongoing gauge of progress. As fitness improves and aerobic power increases, keeping heart rate at the desired level means increasing both the gear and the rpms. The CompuTrainer serves as our mini physiology lab for determining anaerobic threshold and, especially important for mountain-bike riders, maximum power. Maximum power is measured in terms of highest achieved wattage in an all-out sprint that lasts only about 10 seconds.

THE PLAN

For mountain-bike riders, we utilize five training paces that are defined as a percentage of THR. The purpose of this program is to stimulate a physical response in the body. It is important to stimulate the body weekly with at least two of each of these first four categories.

1. **Active recovery**—65 to 70 percent. This range is where you will spend your time between hard efforts without losing fitness. Think of this level as your maintenance pace. Active recovery days are just that: They get the blood flowing but ask little of the body. A typical active recovery looks like this:

30 to 45 minutes of easy low-gear spinning on your mountain bike at 90 to 100 rpms. On a well-dialed road bike those rpms might go up to 120.

2. **Endurance**—75 to 90 percent. Cycling at this level stimulates the body to store glycogen in the muscles. It also accustoms the cyclist's body to the rigors of time in the saddle, and conditions the body's thermal regulatory mechanism to prevent overheating and dehydration.

   The 70s and low 80s end of this range is where you burn fat. Spend 3 to 6 hours spinning at 85 to 90 rpms in small to medium gears and watch the winter roll melt away. Endurance base training can be done once or, preferably, twice per week, followed by active recovery days. I usually do most of my endurance base training (3 to 4 hours per workout) in early January through March, just before the main racing season begins. After the season starts the schedule drops to 1 endurance workout day a week. I suggest you do these on a road bike to save yourself a beating.

3. **AT stimulation**—90 to 100 percent. AT stimulation rides represent the bulk of your primary speed work. Carefully monitor your heart rate and stay in this zone. Riding at or above this level will raise the anaerobic threshold. There is, however, a point of diminishing returns, so respect your limits.

   Use your main racing gear and reduce cadence to a comfortable race level. For most of us this is 75 to 90 rpms. Ten intervals of 3 to 5 minutes with equal-time recovery intervals will do the trick nicely.

4. **VO_2 max stimulation**—100 to 115 percent. Pedaling above VO_2 max will certainly raise maximum oxygen consumption. With patience it will take you to your genetic potential. High-output intervals at this pace with short rests will produce large amounts of lactic acid and increase

your tolerance to lactic buildup. It is not uncommon for fit racers to spend an entire 2-hour race a few ticks above the anaerobic threshold.

I usually do speed work on Tuesdays and Thursdays. I suggest doing your AT stimulation workout on Thursday and the VO_2 max workout on Tuesday, when you are fresher. Again, wear your monitor and stay in the correct zone. Recover with equal-timed rests. Try 12 2-minute intervals. To liven up the workout and recruit both slow- and fast-twitch muscle fibers, try alternating each interval in a slightly higher gear than you would normally use for racing, followed by a lower gear for the next interval.

5. **Speed**—120 percent or more. This level of speed emphasizes very short durations of 20 to 30 seconds. These extremely explosive efforts will promote neuromuscular adaptation and produce maximum speed for short bumps over difficult or technical terrain. The most enjoyable route to this training is with a group of hammerheads at various intervals during the course of one of the other rides. Sprint up steep hills or to predetermined landmarks. Three to 5 such sprints will help you improve both your max power and tactical awareness. Working in this range for short durations will improve your race starts, which, as you know, are usually the key to good races.

GIVE ME 12 WEEKS

That's about how long it will take reasonably fit individuals to achieve substantial results. The first 4 weeks of the building cycle you should commit yourself to riding 4 or 5 days per week. This is your base period. The base is necessary in order to construct a solid aerobic foundation and avoid injury. During this period, ride at the 65 to 70 percent endurance level, cover as many miles in a single workout as is practical, and avoid making multiple stops. Basically, the most important element is time in the saddle.

During the second 4-week period you can drop your time and mileage. On 2 days per week do intervals that are as close as possible to your THR. Warm up well and plan the entire session around a total of 2 hours. These interval days are followed by active recovery days. In order to quantify your results, you may want to do the interval days on a trainer, where you don't have to concern yourself with weather, hills, or traffic. Conditions permitting, do the endurance riding outdoors.

The last 4 weeks of the session are when you will see the greatest return on your investment. The intervals are more difficult and recovery time is shorter. Effort intensity will range from 100 to 110 percent of THR. You should do as many as you can until you see a performance drop of 5 percent. The idea behind these fast intervals and short rests is to produce big-time lactic buildup. By creating large oxygen debts and allowing only enough time for partial recovery, then repeating the cycle, you will change your metabolism to build a greater tolerance to lactic acid.

Below is an example of a typical "hard week" ramp-up from a basic beginner level 3 months earlier.

Monday	Active recovery
Tuesday	AT stimulation
Wednesday	Endurance and weight training
Thursday	AT stimulation

Friday	Active recovery
Saturday	Endurance
Sunday	VO$_2$ max, active recovery

Note: Pay attention to your body. If you find yourself beginning to tire, take 1 to 2 days off to ride easy (active recovery). Usually you need 1 to 2 consecutive days of active recovery every other week.

With the THR training method we have quickly stimulated both VO$_2$ max and AT and developed a usable system for measuring improvements with your heart-rate monitor. Quantifying your progress is really pretty exciting stuff.*

This information is taken from Dave Spangler and Gary Hooker, Cycling Science, March 1990, P.O. Box 1510, Mount Shasta, CA 96067.

All Things Being Equal

Tradition is the last bad performance.

—Arturo Toscanini

STROKE MECHANICS FOR CYCLISTS?

Tom Slocum knows he's right, even as cycling's staid old guard refuses to recognize that anything is wrong. Still, it is troubling to his cadre of faithful followers—something akin to Einstein masked as a plumber, or the Red Baron with clipped ailerons—that his practical genius goes unrewarded.

The theory behind Tom's adjustable cranks makes as much sense as sliced bread when you compare the mechanics of cycling to those of its sister sport, swimming. Even before Johnny Weissmuller was knee high to an ape, swimming coaches were expounding the virtues of good stroke mechanics. How else can we explain that random eight-year-old phenom who, even with no visible muscles, breezes past us in the pool as if we had our suit caught on a lane marker? In our praise of the high-tech, we cyclists have lost touch with a simple fact: Stroke mechanics are as important for us as they are for swimmers. The difference is that swimmers have to correct their strokes with the sweat of labored technique, while we cyclists can literally bolt on our bonus as easily as using an ATM card.

CHAINRINGS AND CRANKS THAT ADDRESS OUR FLAWS

As one who has used both Slocum's leg equalizers and his synchronizer cranks, I can attest to the benefits of balance. The idea is not new: These bodies of ours are not structurally perfect and never have been. We have inconsistent bone lengths and a host of inflexible soft tissues. Instead of enhancing biomechanical efficiency, the standard bicycle drivetrain simply repeats its own mechanical perfection. It does this with crank arms that are lined up with the intended precision of a jackbooted Third Reich marching team.

None of us is perfect. Alexi Grewal, the 1984 Olympic road-racing champion, is not perfect. He had to quit pro racing because his body gave out, but Slocum got him riding again with a set of synchronizers, and now Alexi appears poised for a racing comeback. Chad Gerlach, U.S. postal professional team member, is not perfect either. At the ripe old age of twenty, he was contemplating quitting cycling. His lower back and hips were killing him. "It was just too painful to ride," he remembers. Chad also discovered Slocum, and within a month he was riding pain-free, and stronger than ever before. Team Avocet pro mountain biker Patrick Heaney is another case in point. When Slocum analyzed him, he found unequal leg lengths and, like most of us, uneven muscle firing. After the problem was solved Patrick was retested and realized more than forty watts of extra power with an additional 20 more rpms and reduced recovery times. My own misfiring musculature was advanced just 4 degrees and, whammo, no more dead spot in my stroke; in fact, according to my CompuTrainer Spin Scan program, I've added 15 more watts. That got my attention, especially on top of the extra 20 watts and 30 rpms I had already realized from Slocum's equalizer chainrings, which I'd adopted a year earlier.

In our cycling School of Champions we conduct extensive power testing using Spin Scan, and to date we have found that fewer than 2 percent of all tested athletes pedal with perfect efficiency. The fact remains that few of us are aware that anything is wrong, and even fewer of us have had a Spin Scan stroke analysis.

Many are the advantages of the compound machine. I know plenty of serious swimmers who would give up their birthright to simply bolt on an extra 10 percent of efficiency. Yet despite these available benefits we cyclists are a rather closed-circuit set. Our blinders were lifted, but not removed, a few years ago when pedaling deity Greg LeMond paid the sport of triathlon its biggest tribute. Essentially, Greg gave thanks to his "triathlon handlebars" after winning the Tour de France on the basis of his final Champs-Elysées time trial.

Tom Slocum's equalizers and synchronizers do for biomechanics what tri bars do for aerodynamics. It's a strong statement, and, yes, a few folks may view this information as a commercial pitch since Tom does his analysis in our schools. Still, the facts speak for themselves: Few of us are as efficient as we could be, and change, my fellow athletes, is a fundamental ingredient in the process of personal growth.

WHERE OUR MAKER LEFT OFF . . .

Forget the old adage about all of us being created equal. When it comes to our bodies, most of us are more like works in progress. For cyclists and multisport athletes, even a small difference in leg length can mean decreased horsepower, slower recovery, and, all too often, chronic pain in knees, hips, and backs.

Try pedaling with one leg and notice how the power seems more concentrated from the 2 to 5 o'clock positions of your cranks. This phenomenon is exaggerated in figure 1 by a hypo-

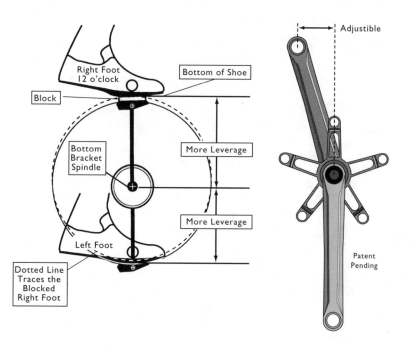

Figure 1. Equalizer chain rings.

Figure 2. Synchronizer crank arms.

thetically shorter right leg. The standard remedy for this problem is a block under the right cleat, as illustrated. Notice the solid line tracing the left shoe and the dotted line indicating the right path. Also note that the only time power is equal is at 3 and 9.

Leverage increases as the distance from the bottom bracket spindle increases. This means that the blocked right foot turns a longer crank at the top of the stroke, thus causing an imbalance. The solution is to keep the block but offset the round chainring. This equalizer chainring increases load as leverage increases, and decreases load as leverage drops. The result is increased power output and far less strain on the lower body. For off-road cyclists this will pay big dividends in terms of fine-tuning a race-winning performance and promoting total recovery between workouts and races.*

*For additional information about Tom's equalizers and synchronizers, contact the School of Champions, 1705 Old Mill Road, Encinitas, CA 92024; (619) 944-3787; Web site: www.interbbs.com/soc/

INDEX

A B O U T   T H E   A U T H O R

J ohn Howard is a NORBA national champion and a personal trainer to numerous road and off-road cyclists and multisport athletes. He is the head coach and director of the School of Champions.

For information about the School of Champions camps, clinics, or personal coaching, write:

The School of Champions
1705 Old Mill Road
Encinitas, CA 92024
phone or fax: (760) 944-3787;
or visit the School of Champions Web site at:
www.interbbs.com/soc/